Joan Rosaire - Lad

Ken Porter - Joan Rosaire

Littoral Press

First Published 2019 by the Littoral Press
15 Harwood Place, Lavenham, Sudbury,
CO10 9SG Suffolk

ISBN 978-1-912412-20-4

British Library Cataloguing-in-Publication Data:
a catalogue record of this book is available from
the British Library

Printed and bound in Great Britain by:
4Edge Ltd. Hockley, Essex
www.4edge.co.uk

JOAN ROSAIRE – LADY OF THE CIRCUS

Contents Page

Acknowledgements and Contributors

Our thanks go out to all those individuals who in some way or another have helped us to write Joan's story. In particular Gaye, Jana, Tracy and Julie who provided us with their memories of the many years they spent working with her.

Special mention must be made of Sylvia Kent for introducing Joan to me, along with Tom Roberts (Robert Bros' Circus) and Michael Austin who were happy to talk to me and David Davis, Honorary Vice President of the Circus Friends Association, who provided me with valuable material. Then there were local colleagues who also provided valuable help. Sue Ranford who wrote a number of the poems for the book, Keith Jackson who has helped improving some of the old photographs. Basildon Borough Heritage who helped with research with special mention of Norman Bambridge who carried out specific research, John and Ann Rugg who painstakingly proof read the manuscript and finally Nigel Pattinson who ran his critical eye over the manuscript.

Special mention must also be made of the inspiration and knowledge received from reading Rupert Croft-Cooke's books on Circus Rosaire and the family – 'The Circus Has no Home' and 'The Happy Highways'.

Where needed we have made every effort to contact the copyright holders of documents or photographs referred to in the book and apologise to anybody not properly acknowledged or who we have not managed to trace.

Foreword

I first met Joan when she was performing with her family's stage circus at the Empire Theatre in York. That was the start of a long friendship, we worked together at the Blackpool Tower Circus, Belle Vue Circus in Manchester, The Hippodrome Circus in Great Yarmouth and many other Venues.

She was an all-round performer but her main love was her horses, she is an extremely good horse lady and her passion for horses is paramount and her animal husbandry is first class, all of her work is done from the heart. I am sure you will enjoy this book; her life story is very interesting.

Norman Barrett – Ringmaster - MBE

Joan and Norman – April 2019

Joan Rosaire – Lady of the Circus

Introduction

It's 12 noon, Thursday 10th August 2017 and I have just left Joan Rosaire who lives at 'Melbourne' Cox's Farm Road, Billericay after spending two fascinating hours with Sylvia Kent (Journalist) and Joan, listening to amazing stories of her circus life. It soon became obvious that Joan's personal life and that of her family's involvement in the circus arena had to be told.

My initial intention was to record her reminiscences of her circus life but she was so enthusiastic from the start that I forgot to switch the recorder on. However, it was soon apparent that I would need to have many meetings with her to get her whole story, which includes being in the presence of Princess Margaret, meeting Princess Anne and appearing with Ken Dodd, Max Bygraves and many other well-known celebrities.

Although I did not record this first meeting, I did leave with a number of photographs, notes and a book 'The Happy Highways' by Rupert Croft-Cooke. This book covers his experience of travelling and living with Joan's mother, uncle and aunts and her grandparents back in the late 1930s with their circus, 'Circus Rosaire'. It is a very interesting and informative book explaining what it was like living in a caravan and preparing for the next show. Unfortunately, an adventure I will not be able to experience but more on Rupert's adventure later.

One of the highlights of the meeting other than Joan's enthusiasm was an old 1960s film she showed us enhanced by one of her cousins of Joan performing in France with her palomino horse Goldy. Joan kept informing us that she had little education but you would never have guessed as she performed this act with Goldy in French. In addition to what Joan had given me at this first meeting I also carried out some preliminary research and was staggered how many references I found of Joan and the circus on the internet and I was a little annoyed because only six months or so earlier I had published a book 'Basildon, Famous People'. It included fifty names of individuals who in their particular field had a connection with Basildon Borough and had become nationally or internationally famous but no Joan. I am sure that as her story unfolds you will agree that she should have been included. I will make sure she appears in the next book on Basildon's Famous and at this point I must again thank Sylvia Kent for introducing me to such an amazing person.

I cannot remember ever going to a live circus, only seeing the various circus acts on television. To my surprise within a week or so of meeting Joan, 'Circus Wonderland' had pitched its tents at Sun Corner Billericay, the same venue that Circus Rosaire performed on many occasions at the start of each circus season.

I decided I must go along to one of the performances to soak up the atmosphere. It was one of Circus Wonderland's regular venues and Joan had been on previous occasions and knew the owners well. She declined on this occasion because she preferred circuses with animals but she was still very complimentary about them.

I went along and purchased tickets for two of my grandchildren and me for a Friday performance and before leaving the ticket office I asked whether they knew Joan. A head popped out from a side office, introduced himself as Paul and said he knew her very well and that she was very famous and a lovely lady. Paul turned out to be Mr Popol the elegant whiteface clown and one of the directors of the circus. He told me to pass on my regards, mentioning she really only preferred circuses with animals.

By the time Friday came the circus had been there for a week but it was still packed. The audience ranged from the very young to the retired and the atmosphere was electric. The following is the opening two paragraphs of their brochure:

'Circus Wonderland is in town, just one stop on an extensive 37 week tour of the UK. From February until November this intrepid troupe of performers will journey 2000 miles to bring

excitement and laughter to 34 different venues, staging 500 performances and attracting attention with 60,000 posters.

The circus is a travelling community, a multi-cultural close-knit family who share the highs and hardships of a life on the road. Clowns, acrobats and aerialist, accompanied by a dedicated team of technicians, drivers and administrators, all coming together to create a spellbinding world of thrills and spills and glitter and glamour, before disappearing again into the night.'

Although it did not have any animals, it certainly had the thrills, spills, glitter, humour and glamour an experience I will not forget. The acts were truly spell binding with performances from artistes from Hungary, Romania, Moldova and Morocco backed up with the humour of the clowns. I will no doubt see them again; you cannot beat a live performance.

'Thank you all so much for entertaining us in Billericay. We visited the show 4 times and our son asked if he could go again. We feel it's so important that children have the opportunity to experience traditional entertainment and Circus Wonderland certainly provides that and more.' John in Billericay

'What a fantastic family night out, my little one has never clapped so much. Great acts and great fun, well worth the money. Thank you Popol, Kakehole, Bertie and the rest of the fabulous circus family.' Sara in Billericay.

As you can gather from the above, I enjoyed my first live circus so within a couple of months I went off and saw 'Russells International Circus' at Rayleigh, Essex. Again, a pleasant experience with different acts. Then another couple of months went by and I went to see the French circus 'Santus Circus' at Sadlers Farm, Bowers Gifford, Essex with my young grandson who lives in France and who was over for a holiday. It had one or two amazing acts. Hegyi Brothers and the Wheel of Death, Romero's Riders and the Globe of Death, a short Laser Light show which was different and I must not forget to mention Batman who the children enjoyed.

I took the liberty to approach a man in a dress suit who looked important, it turned out he was Ernest Santus the ringmaster. He explained that Santus Circus had been visiting the Sadlers Farm site for over twenty years. On asking him whether he knew Joan, his reply was a wonderful lady and that he had had the honour on occasions when he was a young man to help Joan in the ring with her horses when she was performing for Santus Circus.

Though I did not have the opportunity to experience that Rupert Croft-Cooke gained travelling around with Circus Rosaire, I still was able to experience and witness the thrills of the circus performances albeit a different era and no animals. What is also obvious is that just because you have seen one circus it does not mean they are the same year in and year out they all hire in different acts each year and these independent acts move around from one circus to another. This is what Joan did once Circus Rosaire ceased to exist.

I was near to the end of the manuscript after more than a year when I came across a document from the British Library signed by Joan who had given an interview to Barbara Gibson of her memories back in March 2000. Well I could not finish the manuscript until I had listened to the recording. After a few phone calls I managed to arrange to go to the Library and listen to the recordings, six tapes, each of an hour long. I was surprised of how much I had been able to find out about Joan's life from the media, friends and obviously Joan herself. However, these tapes provided me with a little more information or enabled me to embellish on the information I already had. Actually, in the sound archives there were a number of recordings by various circus people under the series 'Oral History of the Circus' one of these recordings was by Joan's uncle, Ivor Rosaire. Unlike these tapes the book will no doubt struggled to get over Joan's humour but hopefully her dedication and love of animals in particular horses will be obvious.

I also decided to contact the Circus Friends Association (CFA) and within days David Davis, Honorary Vice president contacted me and we met up at a service station on the M25. He had first met Joan at the Belle Vue, Manchester sometime in the late 1970s or early 1980s. Although not a circus person himself he had been smitten by the circus, visiting one whenever possible so over the years he and his wife Janice got to know Joan quite well.

He was able to give me a number of King Pole magazines that had articles on Circus Rosaire and Joan along with a number of photographs and programmes. This was followed up a few weeks later with an invitation to Joan and myself by David to join CFA in a celebration organised by Martin Barrett founder of Zippos Circus for Norman Barrett's 21 years with the Circus followed by a Ringmaster's Buffet Lunch and a performance of Zippos Circus.

So, on Easter Saturday, April 20th we made our way to Blackheath where the circus had performed for two weeks in front of large crowds. Timing was perfect because only five days earlier was Joan's 86th birthday. Opposite on the other side of the road was a funfair owned by her cousin Roy Shufflebottom.

I went off and located Norman Barrett's caravan and met him and his wife Sally just to let them know that we had arrived as I know he was expecting us. It was then back to find our seats in a section of the foyer of the Megadome for the proceedings.

At the entrance of the Megadome was Chris Barltrop looking rather grand in his authentic late 1700s ringmaster's dress, possibly similar to what Philip Astley creator of the modern circus wore. Chris had played many roles over the years, Actor, Director, Circus Ringmaster, Event's Organiser and currently publicity officer for Zippos. Joan well remembered Chris as they had originally crossed paths back in the early 1970s. He then showed us into the Buffet area where we sat down and for the next half hour numerous old friends came up and gave Joan a good hug and her special friend Tom Roberts came and sat next to her.

During the celebrations, Norman was presented by David Davis with a small porcelain Budgerigar.

Chris then showed us to seats in the arena. Norman opened the show and finally closed it with his Budgerigar act – Amazing – Joan always goes on about this act. Unfortunately, there were no other animals in the show in particular horses, paperwork had delayed their appearance – EU regulations.

Afterwards it was back to Norman's caravan where Sally had laid on sandwiches etc. We eventually arrived home at 9.30pm after a very enjoyable day.

Within a few weeks of returning from seeing Norman Barrett another lifelong friend Vera called on Joan and took her to see 'Santus Circus' that was back in the area. Though no animals she enjoyed the show very much and again a tremendous fuss was made of her. Vera was a trapeze and juggling artist who had met Joan back in the early days when Joan was performing for Chipperfield Circus. Vera first marriage was to Tommy Fossett. Tommy of the Fossett circus fame and one of their famous clowns, Professor Grimble

Although I had not been able to experience travelling around with a circus, I have certainly enjoyed the experience of meeting and chatting with Joan about her life and there is no doubt that we will continue seeing each other.

'The Circus stands alone as a form of entertainment that reaches the whole family with equal interest. A circus entertainment is as clean as the morning air and as natural to the open country as the foliage and verdure which make for its glory when the circus is due. No man or woman – with a bit of the boy or girl nature left – can fail to respond to the circus show.'

This statement was by a famous writer back in the 1940s and for me is still true today.

If you have never been or taken your children to one may I suggest you do next time one is in your vicinity, I certainly will be going again. There is now no doubt in my mind and I would be very surprised if you didn't love the glittering lights, trapeze artists, clowns etc, with or without its animals and the gay music of the circus.

Although there are numerous references to Joan in the early chapters on the history of Circus Rosaire, her story really begins in chapter 5 “Our Joan with Goldy”.

THE CIRCUS IS COMING TO TOWN

Posters go up all over the town,
The circus is heading this way.
Excitement mounts in the schools around
As the children count down the days.

The open road is the life they chose,
Travelling from town to town,
Always meeting new people,
Not knowing where they're bound.

The Lorries and trailers are packed and ready
Laden with heavy loads.
They drive in convoy down the lanes
And onto our busy roads.

They stumble into the farmer's field
A strange, exotic sight.
The animals are fed and watered
And settled for the night.

Early next morning the Big Top appears,
Guy ropes keeping it steady.
The seating is in position
And the circus is almost ready.

By Sue Ranford (Basildon Borough Heritage Society)

The Final question, what were we going to call the book, 'Joan Rosaire and Wonder horse Goldy' No, so we thought of adding 'Circus Queens' No, as this would be slightly misleading as it was only the original Goldy that was a mare? 'Horse will travel', Joan always thinks of her horses' first, but again No, as it does not really give an indication that the book is about her career in the circus. Then her cousin Ralph from next door suggested 'Joan Rosaire made/maid in the Circus'. There is no doubt that Joan's career was made/forged in the circus and we nearly went with this one. Then we realised that Norman Barrett had mention she was a lady so it had to be 'Joan Rosaire – Lady of the Circus'.

Chapter 1 – Origins of the Modern Circus

The glamour of the circus as we know it has mesmerised audiences across the world for over 200 years and with their daring acts, skill and humour it has been the making of household names for many circus performers. Joan is one of them but before we embark on her story, I feel we must have a quick look at the history of the circus. The dictionary tells us that the word circus is derived from the Latin word 'circle'. So, the mind immediately jumps back to Roman times with their Amphitheatres and Circuses which in practice were an improvement on the Greek stadiums.

A well-known Roman Circus was *Circus Maximus* in Rome, a long, narrow, U-shaped structure designed for chariot races. Their Amphitheatres were large, circular or oval, open-air structures with raised seating. They were used for events such as gladiator combats, chariot races, animal slayings and executions; another well-known amphitheatre was the Colosseum in Rome. To date we have established that there were ten amphitheatres in Britain, Silchester, Chester, St Albans and Chichester being possibly the most well-known. London was another but not discovered until 1998 under Guildhall. The latest one to be found is at Colchester discovered in 2005. After the fall of Rome, amphitheatres survived for some time before falling into disuse along with the spectacles that they held and it was going to be another 1000 years before similar structures were going to re-appear with spectator events such as the knightly tournaments of the Middle Ages in Europe.

Though the question continually being asked is whether the history of the circus actually dates back to Roman times, many believe not and that the Roman circus was actually the precursor of the modern racetrack. If this is so the only connection between Roman and modern circuses as already mentioned is the word, *circus,* which in Latin and in English means, *'circle,'* with circus in Latin meaning '*ring, circular line*' probably adapted from the ancient Greek word '*Kirkos*' meaning *circular*.'

Acrobats, clowns, trained animals, trick riders' familiar components of the circus environment have in fact existed throughout history and during the medieval age groups of entertainers travelled from village to village entertaining the village people with their songs and storytelling and they became known as minstrels. By the 17th century Country Fairs began to spring up throughout England and this enabled the various performers to show off their talent. Acrobats, jugglers, dancers and riding exhibitions became regular fixtures. Then in the late 18th century the modern circus appeared. It was created and performed in London in 1768 by Philip Astley, a former Cavalry Sergeant Major who had served in the Seven Years War (1756-63) as part of Colonel Elliott's 15th Light Dragoons regiment. He had built up a reputation as a horse-breaker and trainer and on his discharge decided to put his experience to good use. The Colonel now a General presented Philip with a white charger named Gibraltar. On discharge in 1766, Philip found work in a riding school in Islington before opening up his own riding school in 1768 at Halfpenny Hatch. He was an expert in trick riding and it was soon obvious to him that trick riders received considerably more attention from the public. So, in the morning he would teach people the basic skills of horsemanship and in the afternoon would perform his feats of horsemanship on Gibraltar. He also exhibited a small horse he called 'The Little Military Horse' who he had trained to add and subtract numbers, feign death, fire a pistol and perform mind-reading tricks. He also discovered that if he galloped in a tight circle, centrifugal force allowed him to perform seemingly impossible feats on horseback. His wife Patty also took an active role and in addition to collecting the entrance fees and performing drum-rolls she often performed riding tricks.

His first performance was on 9 January 1768, whereby he formed a ring and invited the public to see him ride a horse with one foot on the saddle, the other on the horse's head waving a sword in the air. By 1770 he had purchased a timber yard nearby at Westminster Bridge Road, London, his trick riding received such favourable response that his success had outshone his reputation as a teacher. He followed this success up by hiring other equestrians, clowns, musicians, acrobats, rope-dancers and jugglers etc. One must be mindful that these additional artists as mentioned had performed throughout Europe for centuries but as members of independent professions and not part of an integrated group. In 1770 he built a roof over his ring and called the structure Astley's Amphitheatre.

His original ring size was about sixty-two feet in diameter but it was eventually scaled down to forty-two feet, which has become the international standard for all circus rings. Of course, one of the great advantages of the ring was that the spectators could see what was going on which would have been more or less impossible if the horse riders were forced to gallop in a straight line. So, with the combination of equestrian displays and other entertaining acts it is no wonder that Philip Astley is regarded as being the father of the 'modern circus.' Although he did not adopt the name circus, this was down to one of his competitors.

Astley's Amphitheatre by August Pugin & Thomas Rowlandson – Houghton

In 1772 a former member of Astley's company, equestrian Charles Hughes opened up his own riding school not far away on Blackfriars Road. Although competition between them became fierce it did generate considerable interest and therefore good business. Hughes took his show round Europe for the next eight years before returning to London in 1781 where he went into partnership with a songwriter and author of pantomimes, Charles Dibdin. They opened up a rival amphitheatre and riding school calling their amphitheatre 'The Royal Circus and Equestrian Philharmonic Academy.' It was Charles Dibdin who came up with the name 'circus' and it was not long before the name was adopted for this new form of entertainment.

In the meantime, Astley in 1772 was invited to perform his feats of horsemanship before King Louis XV in Versailles. The response was such that in 1782 he opened his first Paris circus, '*Amphitheatre Anglais.*' His son John was also involved and on occasions this allowed two performances to run concurrently, one in London and one in Paris. Things now started to take off in a big way and during times he was not performing in London he was touring and establishing wooden amphitheatres throughout Great Britain. It soon won him the nickname 'Amphi-Philip.' Dublin, Ireland in 1773 was the first. In 1779 he took on the title of Equestrian Director – today's ringmaster. He went on to build a total of nineteen different circuses in various European capitals. He never used wild animals in his shows.

Astley died on 20 October 1814, aged seventy-two at his second home, Rue du Faubourg du Temple, Paris and is buried at Mount-Louis Cemetery, Paris. He had become a legend in his own life time. Astley and his Amphitheatre have been mentioned in the popular fiction of Charles Dickens, Jane Austen and William Thackeray and others. At least three dance tunes have his name – '*Astley's Rides,*' '*Astley's Flag*' and '*Astley's Hornpipe.*' Also, the circus is featured in Tracy Chevalier's novel '*Burning Bright.*' Finally, Andrew Van Buran commissioned a life size statue of Astley by sculptor Andrew Edwards and in November 2005 it was unveiled at the Newcastle-under-Lyme College's Performing Arts Centre, Newcastle being Astley's birthplace.

Astley was followed by Andrew Ducrow who became the proprietor of Astley's Amphitheatre and is credited with being the originator of horsemanship acts, his most famous act being the 'Courier of St Petersburg.' The performance consists of a rider straddled across two cantering horses through which a courier would pass on his way to Russia between the horses and under his legs, while other horses bear the flags of the various countries, it was the forerunner of modern horse acts and is still performed with variations today at equestrian events. His feats of horsemanship had a lot to do with establishing the traditions of the circus and it is no wonder he was often called the 'Father of British circus equestrianism.'

This form of entertainment had grasped the imagination of the people and was beginning to progress at a considerable pace. Charles Hughes in 1793 performed at the court of Catherine the Great in St Petersburg, Russia and then in the same year one of his former pupils John Ricketts opened the first circus in Philadelphia, America. George Washington was seen at a performance some three months after it opened. Four years later in 1797 he went on to open the first Canadian Circus in Montreal.

For a time, his only competition came from another British equestrian Philip Lailson who had followed him to the United States in 1795. He went on to open up in Mexico in 1802. The expansion in America was rapid especially during the first two decades of the 19th century, for example the Circus of Pepin and Brechard toured from Montreal to Havana and later Purdy, Welch & Co and Van Amburgh helped to spread the popularity of the circus in the United States.

Initial circus performances were held in static buildings, although they were often temporary wooden structures but it was not long before every major European and the largest New World cities had at least one permanent arena. Then in 1825 Joshua Purdy Brown became the first circus owner to replace the wooden structures with a large tent. This enabled him to set up and take down more easily, making it possible for him to move from location to location every day if necessary, therefore attracting a larger audience from the wilds of America. However, it was Nathan Howes a year later who added the big top to the circus tent enabling performances to take place in any weather. Though it could be said that England was the birth place of the modern circus, it was however, America who gave us the iconic and enduring image of the big top. It was also around this time that Van Amburgh introduced wild animals to the circus scene.

Although the collection of captive animals kept for displays can be traced back to Roman times, such collections were known as Menageries. Travelling menageries became very popular at fairs etc. during the 18th and 19th Century and as stated Van Amburgh introduced wild animals to the circus scene in America in the 1820s, and by the mid-1830s menageries became a large part of the circus scene. The British equestrian Thomas Cooke in 1836 brought back from America to England the travelling circus tent (The Big Top) and it was not long afterwards that wild animals were appearing in British circuses, but it was not only in America and England that circuses were expanding. They were expanding all over Europe and the rest of the world, the Italian equestrian Giuseppe Chiarini for some forty years travelled the world with his circus, North and South America, Mexico, Chile, Argentina, China and Brazil. He also toured Australia, New Zealand, Tasmania, Singapore, Java, Siam and India. There were many others, Jacques Tourniaire, French equestrian established the first Russian circus in 1816. There was however a lull in America during the civil war. Then in 1870 Phineas Taylor Barnum established a travelling circus called 'P.T.Barnum's Grand Travelling Museum, Menagerie, Caravan & Hippodrome. In 1881 he merged with James Bailey and James Hutchinson and the show became known as the 'Greatest Show on Earth' before being shortened to 'Barnum & Bailey'. Finally, after several ups and downs it became known as 'Barnum & Bailey Circus' and toured the world.

Poster

The following is P.T.Barnum's slogan for his circus in 1881: -
'Jugglers, grease paint, drum-rolls, implausible moustaches, gunpowder, outsize shoes, lions, ompah music, spangly acrobat. Such extraordinary goings-on under the big top

have a special resonance for us all. They're as much a part of the British childhood experience as conkers, seaside holidays and Blue Peter and quite rightly, because the circus we know today was fashioned by a trick-riding English cavalryman called Sergeant Major Philip Astley in the 1760s.

Although some of the individual acts were familiar to earlier audiences, notably in ancient Rome, Astley concluded that a show combining displays by horses, acrobats, trapeze artists, tight-rope walkers and - everyone's favourite - clowns, would be an unmissable spectacular.

So, next time you see a striped big top and hear the roar of the crowd, spare a thought for a long departed English cavalry officer who gave us 'The Greatest Show on Earth.' These words would not go amiss on any circus programme today.

Barnum died in 1902 causing Bailey to return to the United States where he faced serious competition from the Ringling Brothers who on Bailey's death in 1906 purchased Barnum & Bailey. The circus finally closed down after more than 100 years in operation in May 2017. The main cause appears to be the owners phasing out the elephant acts due to the mounting criticism from animal rights groups.

Barnum's most famous Elephant was his Giant African elephant Jumbo whom he had purchased from London Zoo for £2000 in 1882. He exhibited Jumbo for the first time at Madison Square Gardens and within three weeks had recouped the purchase price. For the next three years travelling around America and Britain Jumbo became the circus's main attraction. Unfortunately, in September 1885 Jumbo was struck and killed by a locomotive. In 1985 on the centennial of the Elephant's death a life-size statue was erected in St Thomas, Ontario, Canada.

Now, what about Buffalo Bill's 'Wild West Show' - was it a circus or a travelling variety show? The show opened on 19 May 1883 in Omaha Nebraska. William F Cody (Buffalo Bill) had been in the show business, staging shows known as 'border dramas' featuring genuine frontier characters, real Indians, fancy shooting including horses for a decade or more before going out on the road with his acts.

Jumbo Statue in St Thomas, Ontario
photo by Einor Einarsson Kvaran

In the next thirty odd years he took his show around the world with many well-known Wild West characters; Wild Bill Hickok, Annie Oakley, Calamity Jane, Geronimo, Chief Sitting Bull to name a few.

The shows consisted of historical re-enactments, such as 'Custer's Last Stand' or the 'Battle of Little Big Horn' (25 June 1876) combined with displays of sharp shooting and rodeo style events such as cowboys trying to rope and ride broncos. Broncos being unbroken horses, they would also attempt to try and ride mules, buffalos, steers, elk, deer, bears and moose. Each show would begin with a parade on horseback, with a band playing in the background.

Although by the mid-nineteenth century America seemed to be leading the way in this form of entertainment the rest of the

World was doing their bit, with more and more death-defying feats, wild animals and larger-scale performances including Wild West shows. They were still going strong in the twentieth century considering the number of ups and downs partly due to world conflicts they had to endure. In fact, the circus had come to represent a close-knit community that offered the opportunity for performers a chance to travel the world.

We cannot bypass Europe in the history of the circus and one of the main contributors that jumps to mind is Circus Knie. It all started with Austrian Friedrich Knie (1754-1850). At a young age he became a travelling entertainer and in the early 1800s he formed his own company of rope-dancers and the Knie Arena came into being. It travelled around Austria then Germany and finally in 1814 Switzerland. It developed into a successful and reputable enterprise in these three countries. Friedrich died on the 3 February 1850 in Berthoud, Switzerland but by then the Knie Dynasty had been formed.

Karl one of his sons took over the business and it continued to prosper. It gave a varied show, with acrobats, jugglers, rope acts and comedy scenes but his reign was short lived as he died unexpectedly in December 1860 but his wife and other members of his family kept the Arena going. By now the family were beginning to feel at home in Switzerland but with the various conflicts going on in Europe it took until December 1900 before the family obtained Swiss citizenship. World War One brought more difficulties for the Knie Arena and restricted their travels mainly to Switzerland. After the war the four great great grandchildren of Friedrich, - Rudolf, Karl, Eugen and Friedrich Jr. - decided to transform the Arena into a fully-fledged tenting circus. Circus Knie opened on 14 June 1919 in Bern, Switzerland and in 1920 Friedrich Jr. brought horses into the circus. His two sons (5th Generation) Friedrich, known as Freddy and Rudolf known as Rolf both made their circus debut as acrobats when they were four years old.

The Second World War again caused the circus problems restricting their travelling to Switzerland but after the war they bounced back and today they are into the 7th and 8th generations of the Knie Dynasty which is maintaining a unique position in Europe. It is still performing with animals and is proud of the animal care it provides in a time when many circuses are having a hard time adapting to the public's change of sensitivity regarding the way animals are being treated and kept with travelling circuses. So, the circuses were holding their own in America and Europe so what was going on in Britain? Well it has been said that no British story is complete without a mention of 'Lord' George Sanger. George had obtained the nick name 'Gentleman George' from fellow showmen but his father called him 'his Lordship' because of the smart way he dressed. It was George Sanger who is credited with bringing the flair and showmanship of the fairground to the circus and making it part of the mass entertainment culture.

He was born in 1825 in Newbury, Berkshire and as a young man started his own business as an animal tamer. His first group of animals or 'troupe' being the correct term were canaries, redpolls (small finch), white mice and hares. Somehow, he taught them to fire miniature cannons and walk tightropes. His private shows were a success so with his brothers William and John they started up a travelling show including conjuring. Then in 1848 they took the show to Stepney Fair where he met a childhood friend, Ellen Chapman, who he married in 1850 in Sheffield. She was a professional lion tamer known as Madame Pauline de Vere and had been performing with Wombwell's circus. Following several years of success at the Stepney Fair the brothers decided in 1854 to form a circus, their first purchase being a Welsh pony and the next six years they toured the United Kingdom. By 1858 they had six lions and the largest stud of horses in Europe. It is understood that by 1860 the Sanger Circus was visiting over two hundred towns during a nine-month season. This included two shows a day with the exception of Sunday. The logistics of moving the circus every day must have been a nightmare to organise including at least ten wagons to carry the tenting equipment, a lamp wagon, eight or ten living carriages, a foal wagon, ten wild beast wagons full of lions, tigers, bears etc, a harness wagon, a portable blacksmith's forge, property wagons, wardrobe and dressing wagons, a band carriage and finally at least six great tableau cars for the circus parade – once on the road the train of wagons unbelievably covered nearly two miles.

Due to their success they purchased Astley's Amphitheatre in 1871 which they continued to run until 1893. At around the same time they purchased the Agricultural Hall in Islington. Their circus business boomed but the two brothers decided to split up, it was an amicable arrangement. John travelled Britain with his own circus, while George in addition to touring Britain also decided in 1874 to try his luck on the continent which he did for the next fifteen years. It was also not long before John was also calling himself 'Lord' John Sanger. During this time George purchased land in Margate and built an entertainment centre and menagerie called 'The Hall by the Sea' with Brother William managing it. He also built an Amphitheatre in Ramsgate, Kent in 1893. George retired in 1905, then six years later the unbelievable happened, he was murdered by one of his employees Herbert Charles Cooper who attacked him with a hatchet and then committed suicide.

Although Lord George Sanger's circus was one of the largest in Britain at the time, it had by the 1950s reverted to a small two-pole tented show, playing for short periods in small towns. It was kept on the road by the Freeman family who had been associated with Sanger Circus and others for a considerable time. It was Victoria Sanger Freeman the great granddaughter of 'Lord' George Sanger and her brother George Sanger who kept the circus going until it closed in 1962 bringing to an end 117 years of Sanger circus. (John's circus had ceased just before the Second World War). Like many other circus performers, she had appeared in many other circuses, for example she performed for the first two or three years of the Bertram Mills Circus at Olympia, West London. In fact in those early years the Sanger family provided the nucleus of the Mills performances.

As we move further into the twentieth century it is the big three that readily come to mind. Chipperfield's, Bertram Mills and Billy Smart.

Charles Chipperfield's Circus is still performing around the country and is the 7th generation of the Circus family. They can trace their pedigree back to James Chipperfield who first performed with animals at the Thames Frost Fair in 1684. Then throughout the 19th Century, the circus toured all over England with its animals, acrobats and clowns. During the 1950s it became one of the largest circuses in Europe with a big top that could accommodate 6000 people. It had a collection of 200 horses, 16 elephants and 200 other animals. Their biggest rivals were Bertram Mills and Billy Smart.

Bertram Mills was born in August 1893. He enlisted into the Royal Army Medical Corps at the beginning of World War 1, rising to the rank of Captain. On leaving the army he became interested in the circus world and in 1920 he had formed a new circus company 'Bertram Mills International Circus.' After appearing for the first time at Olympia on the 17 December 1920 it was not long before it became a touring circus. It was patronized on many occasions by the Royal Family. Following his death in 1938 his sons Bernard and Cyril continued the circus success until the 1960s. The circus was finally disbanded due to increased competition from television.

Billy Smart was showman and fairground proprietor who in 1946 bought a second-hand circus tent and equipment, believed to be from Cody's circus. He ran initially a small circus called 'New World Circus' in conjunction with his fun fair. It proved very popular and by the early 1950s it expanded into a big top with seating capacity of around 6,000. It also had a vast entrance tent that enabled the staging of spectacular parades which became part of the circus trademark.

Where Billy was particularly successful was his involvement with the newly established television. He agreed in 1947 to have his circus televised. This continued with the BBC and became the 'Billy Smart's Christmas Spectacular'. ITV took it over in 1979 until 1982. The circus became one of the largest in the World and by 1960, its menagerie carried more than 40 horses, 15 elephants and a large variety of exotic and wild animals. He died in his caravan on the 25 September 1966, soon after conducting the Romford Boy's Band in a tent at Ipswich.

Photograph by Daniel Hill

Billy Smart Jr. and Brothers Ronald and David took over the running of the circus but it stopped touring in 1971 and although Ronald and nephew Gary revived it in 1993, it did not survive very long.

Cody's Circus was a small circus run by Harry Cody. He had one big elephant, three lions, a few horses, ponies, monkeys and dogs. It would appear that in the early 1950s Cody had intended to retire but in fact continued for a time in the West Country and the circus did not disappear until a decade later.

While the big three were touring and competing against each other a Norman Barrett was making his way and there were a number of smaller circuses coming and going but also doing a great job, Fossett's Circus, Pool Brothers, Madame Paulo's, The Miller Brothers Australian Circus, James Roberts, Jack Hiltons, Cottle and Austin, Volpre's Circus, Sandow, Tom Arnold, Gandey and Santus circus to name a few and of course Joan's grandparent's Circus, 'Circus Rosaire.'

Norman Barrett over many years has become the most loved and best-known circus personality in Britain. He is known as the 'Lord of the Ring.' In 1990 he appeared in the favourite TV show, 'This is your Life' at the Blackpool Tower. Our Joan was one of the Guests but disappointedly not Goldy. In 2010 he was made a Member of the British Empire (MBE), an extremely rare distinction from the world of the circus. Then in 2011 he was inducted into the International Circus Hall of Fame and one of the best comments made about him was from Ken Dodd, the legendary comedian: 'A smashing bloke and a very very nice man….A loyal friend and a very very very nice man.'

Norman was born in York, England in 1935, his parents George and Winifred were at the time taking a break from their circus life. George had previously purchased a farm (Low Farm), which had a stock of farm animals, dogs, geese, ponies and even a fox which he started to train. In 1924 they met up with the travelling Rosaire circus which was visiting the village of Bishop Wilton, east of York. Fred and Florence Rosaire (Ross) were performing under the name of Desmonds when George went across to see their show as he was keenly interested in dogs, horses and all kinds of animals. George notably impressed, invited Fred Ross who later became famous throughout Circusdom as 'Count Rosaire,' to visit the farm and see his performing horses.

The immediate result was that the Rosaire family spent the winter at George's farm. Not surprisingly George became increasingly interested in the circus and eventually Fred suggested that they should go into partnership and take out a tenting circus together.

According to Norman Barrett's autobiography they practised all winter, using a ring in the covered fold yard, with a 'mechanic' rigged for riding practice. This consisted of a pulley fixed over the centre of the ring, through which is led a strong rope. One end of the rope is a broad waistband which is buckled round the trainee rider while the other end is held by one or two helpers so that if the rider, learning to stand on the rump of a moving horse, for example should lose their balance or footing, the assistants would heave the rider into the air to prevent a fall and possible injury.

By early 1925 they were ready and the new circus opened up in Ouseburn under the name of 'Desmond and Barrett's Amalgamated Monster Circus', later moving on to Hampton (Ring O' Bells) on 2 June 1925. George was the equestrian director and the general manager was 'F Desmond (Ross).

The Rosaire family's contribution to the programme included The Desmond Family on the aerial rings; Derrick the Lightning Rodeo Bareback Rider; Dennis on the silver wire; Zenoto (Zena) the Flexible Boneless Wonder and the three Rosaros, acrobats. George's equestrian offerings included Sultan and Jackie in 'Dignity and Impudence;' the four spotted liberty horses; Cinders the 'spotted retrieving pony of remarkable intelligence' and 'Firefly,' a most wonderful Waltzing and Trick Jumping Entire Horse, a horse that our Joan was many years later to have the opportunity to ride. The tent seated upwards of 1,000.

Unfortunately, the partnership did not last long and by the end of June they parted company, dividing the equipment with the tent going to the Rosaires. When George parted company with the Rosaires they formed their own Barrett's Canadian Circus. The circus closed down in 1931 but was resurrected in 1948 and again in 1952. At the age of seventeen Norman was presenting horses and a team of dogs at the circus. In the same year his father sold the circus and it started a period of Norman moving around from circus to circus. He initially worked for circuses such as Robert Gandey's Circus and Cody's Circus and as a clown presented geese and helped his future first wife Sue Yelding (another family steeped in Circus history) with her dog act.

In 1956 he moved with the Yeldings to the Robert Brothers Circus at the time one of Britain's largest tenting circuses and it was here his career as a ringmaster began. Ringmaster is the name given today to the old position of

Equestrian Director. Robert Brothers along with Billy Smarts were the two main circuses that appeared on the television during the 1950/60s. Norman's big chance in circus show business came in 1959 when he joined the Bertram Mills Circus as an assistant animal trainer and presenter. This followed with work with Belle Vue International Circus and Blackpool Tower with Chipperfield's Circus. For the winter of 1961-62 he became one of Bertram Mills Equestrian Directors and soon established himself as Master of the Ring. 1964 saw him officiating as Bertram Mills Ringmaster for their last tenting season but he moved on for three years with their circus at Olympia. He also found time to hone his skills with Circus Scott, Sweden's premier circus. Then in 1966 he began a long association with the Blackpool Tower Circus.

His time at the Tower Circus ended in 1990 when the owners banned animals and he moved on to the newly formed Superdome Circus nearby where he continued to present a traditional circus with animals including his own act with his budgerigars. In between he travelled to Europe and America with his birds also appearing on the TV. He last tented with Circus Scott in Sweden before settling down with Zippo's Circus as ringmaster in the later part of twentieth century and is still going strong today. Zippo's with its animals was established in 1970 by Martin Burton and today is acknowledged as Britain's largest and best circus.

Norman's employer Martin Burton has stated: - 'Norman, with his inimitable style and showmanship, is recognized across the globe as the world's greatest living ringmaster.'

It might be the animals and acrobats that thrill the audiences but there is no doubt that comedy has played a very big part of circus life from its very early days. Initially this was in the form of the comic horsemanship but it was not long before the circus clown came into his own. Clowning was at first one of all-round skills, tumbling and riding either as part of a featured act or entertaining the audiences and children in particular with a form of slapstick while the next act was getting ready. They also act as ring assistants, holding balloons and ribbons for the riders to leap through and over, engaging in a little repartee with the audience to give the various acts breathing space.

There have been many great clowns, Joseph Grimaldi for instance a great English actor (Russian by birth) clown of the early 19th Century. He was one of the first, if not the first to paint geometric patterns on his face. In his honour and memory all clowns are affectionately known as 'Joeys.' His costumes and make-up were copied by Andrew Ducrow and many circus clowns.

1900 Postcard

Then probably one of the most famous clowns in the UK during the middle decades of the 20th century was none other than

Coco (Nicolai Poliakoff). Nicolai was born on 5 October 1900 to a poor Jewish family in Dvinsk (today Daugavpils), Latvia. At the age of eight he ran away and joined a circus. He was placed in the care of a clown and acrobat, Vitaly Lazarenko. He returned home a few years later but persuaded his father to allow him to follow a circus career. He was apprenticed for four years to Rudolfe Truzzi, with whom he studied the fundamentals of acrobatics, trapeze, horse riding and an array of circus disciplines.

After the First World War and the Civil War in Russia he travelled widely in the Soviet Union and Europe, eventually joining the Bertram Mills Circus on 21 December 1929 which turned out to be an association of thirty-seven years. He and his wife Valentina became British citizens on 21st October 1949. He appeared on Eamonn Andrews 'This is Your Life' programme in 1962 and was awarded the OBE in 1963 for services to road safety among children. He died on the 25 September 1974.

I feel I should however also mention Allan Dixon, why because it was Circus Rosaire that gave him the opportunity at the age of eleven back in 1954. Allan at the time was attending Henderson Avenue Junior School, Scunthorpe when in January of the year the circus was performing at the Savoy Theatre. He was truly smitten and he spent every night backstage talking to the performers including his future boss and mentor Dennis Rosaire. Dennis spotted the potential of this 3ft 9in lad who was to grow no more than 4ft. A week later, the clown in the making said goodbye to his family and joined the circus. It was going to be four years before he returned.

Allan was determined to make the circus his career but it was at least twelve months before he was allowed to take an official part in entertaining. Before then he was kept busy training for his 'act' which included clowning around with performing geese, performing on the trampoline, later he would slide through a sea of shaving foam and paint - it was pure slapstick.

Over the next fifty years as he moved around the world performing for many circuses, he met a number of well-known people including two Popes, Paul and John Paul 11, Prince Rainier, Princess Grace, Kirk Douglas, Diana Dors, Dirk Bogarde and many other film stars. He returned to his home town Scunthorpe following retirement in 2007. He passed away in June 2017 at the age of 74.

On the 14 September 2018 members of the Zippos Circus including Norman Barrett MBE unveiled a flagstone in the front garden of St Thomas' Hospital at the southern end of Westminster Bridge being the site of the world's first circus amphitheatre at Halfpenny Hatch. The inscription reads: -

'Here stood Astley's Royal Amphitheatre: The world's first circus building: Celebrating the invention of the modern circus by Riding Master Philip Astley in 1768: Commemorative stone laid September 2018: Donated by Zippos Circus, London's favourite circus.'

Photograph by David Davis and Janice Fisk

Chapter 2 - Day in the Life of a Circus

The following is a day in the life of a modern travelling circus, penned a few years ago by Joan: -

'What constitutes a normal day for them? Let us for a while assume the life of a circus artist - what shall we be - a wire walker perhaps, or maybe a clown, better still - let us aspire to be the ringmaster himself!

So, our day begins early, perhaps not quite as early as the grooms who care for the animals though, their charges must be watered, fed, cleaned out and where necessary, groomed ready for practice. You and I will collect the mail from the Booking Office which is the 'hub' of the management in our world. We will see if there is to be any change in the programme, find out if any more sawdust is required to be put in the ring, make sure the ring grooms' uniforms are in good order - if not designate someone to take dirty items to be laundered. Maybe the ring fence will need a coat of white emulsion and the carpet that is put down in the ring centre for the acrobats will require sweeping (was there a suspicion of dirt on it at last night's performance?). Meanwhile the circus is wakening, by now the aroma of coffee will be wafting seductively around the various caravans, we may be invited to partake of some at any number of them, today we choose to have coffee with the lion trainer and his family, who recently had an increase in their brood, two lion cubs were born to a young lioness, who for reason only known to herself, has discarded one of them. So, it is now the task of the lion trainer's wife to rear it along with the rest of her family. This she will do happily enough, for there is nothing quite as enchanting as a baby lion, albeit it will take as much of her time as a human baby for the first three months.

Next, we will go to the performers' entrance and check that the props (the artist's accoutrements) are all in order, each artist is responsible for his own props but our job is just to see that everything is correct and in good order. Now we will stop awhile and watch the liberty horses being given a run through, a new trick is being introduced and will require quite a bit of practice. The jingle of harness and snorts of the horses mingle with the trainer's voice as he speaks soothingly or gives a sharp command.

As much as we would like to linger here, we must press on, for "press" being the operative word. Today the local paper is sending a reporter and we must arrange for the clowns to be in costume for a photograph, later the same clowns will be attending the local school for more publicity. Before we leave the tent, we will look on the notice board to see if there has been any lost property reported, this will be handed in at the booking office. The times allotted for practice in the ring are also written up here. Usually the horses and elephants have first go, followed by the ground acts (acrobats - spring board balancing) flying trapeze etc. lastly the cage acts, the cage will then be left for the exercise of the wild beasts, until just before the first performance.

As we make our way through the big top, someone tells us of a leak in the stand pipe that gives us water, this must be fixed, we will arrange with the mechanic to fix this. His job is to maintain the vehicles on the show but this would also be one of his duties. We see the head stable groom, he hails us and says he is running out of straw, could we arrange for some more for the morning and better quality. Also, the boy who looks after the wild beasts wants some more porridge oats and vegetables for the bears and monkeys and one of the barrier fences in the menagerie needs attending to at once, before the public are admitted - this will also come under the auspices of the mechanic who is among other things an experienced welder, the show carries most of its own equipment to repair and refurbish, as it is practically impossible to get things done at short notice locally, whilst travelling.

We have to see the tent master about some new rigging wanted by the flying trapeze act, it is his job along with the rigger in the act to see this is fixed when actually erecting the big top. The wardrobe mistress says one of the ring groom's overalls is absolutely beyond repair and could we please take more care in future! The wardrobe lady just happens in this case to be the wife of the clown, who will be doing this morning's publicity, so here we kill two birds with one stone by telling her where she has to go today and what time she may be expected back for his meals - speaking of which we will look in on the grooms cook house about a complaint made by one of the grooms, he says his food is always cold and the cook says he is always late!

By lunch time things are getting a bit hectic. A part for one of the Lorries cannot be found locally, so somebody must drive to another town to try purchase it. It has been decided that the mechanic's assistant who also doubles as a programme seller will have to go, so we must find a replacement for him this afternoon. Selling programmes is very important, for the revenue helps to pay for the circus advance publicity, which tends to be expensive.

The publicity crew are the ones who go ahead of the show and arrange for bills to be put up on hoardings, adverts in the local papers, town travel agents to book seats for the performances, arrange for fodder to be delivered, electricity supply, phone and water to be put on when the circus arrives. Sometimes a deposit must be paid on the site, which will be forfeited if the ground is left less than spotless. They also have to give out hand bills plus any other publicity needed, they are a very necessary part of the circus but seldom are actually seen on the show itself, though if anything goes wrong, it is traditional to treat them to all the blame!

These days the circus children have a tutor who travels with the circus but in addition to his schoolroom duties often does other office duties - our teacher this afternoon will be asked if he will replace the programme seller. So, as we look in on the school teacher in the school caravan we hear the chanting of a poem, but as we listen more closely, we find it is not just a rhyme but an ancient circus monologue: -

"This morn I arose
From sweet repose -
I goes out among the trees that grows
To shoot some crows -
I meet one of my foes -
We have some words that quickly
Comes to blows -
He hits me on the nose and down I goes -
Into the gutter where the dirty water flows -
Up I arose, off home I goes
I takes off my wet clothes
And into bed I goes
I turn up my toes
I tallows up my nose
I has a sweet repose
And that's all I knows."

Unknown Author

Lead vehicle to let people know that the circus is coming to town.

It's getting near to the first performance time and we still have a few things left to do. We must remember to see if the sawdust was put in the ring so that it looks fresh, also mustn't forget to collect our white breeches from the wardrobe lady, who has been kind enough to sew on some buttons that were getting loose. By now all the animals will have been groomed, exercised and prepared for their first appearance, the box office staff hopefully will have been busy selling tickets in advance.

The various wives of artists and personnel will have been busy shopping, cooking, washing etc. for there is quite a little village of its own on a circus. The 'Boss' will want to see us just before show time, so that he can check every detail in order to ensure everything goes without a hitch.

Now it's time for us to get into our costume and blow the first whistle - this is the signal for half an hour before we begin, there will be one blast for the half hour, two blasts for the quarter hour, and then three blasts for five minutes. Overture and beginners will all be assembled in the back entrance by the third whistle or they will be reprimanded, if they are late, a second time, a fine will be imposed. Fortunately, this seldom happens, most artists are already in the back entrance warming up long before their respective acts.

Well the big moment has arrived, the tent is packed the audience waiting, the overture has been played, the curtains open and with a deep breath in we go,

"Ladies and Gentlemen" rings out the voice of our ring master. He stands in the centre of the ring bathed in a spotlight, resplendent in his red tail coat, spotless white breeches, immaculate boots, magnificent shining silk top hat held in one hand. "You are about to witness a spectacle that will dazzle your eyes - a veritable feast of wonder and excitement never before equaled in the history of mankind. We will present to you a program that will gladden your heart and live long in your memory as being the very "Time of Your Life." So now without further ado, "ON WITH THE SHOW!"

It's now his job to not only announce each act but to make sure all the "props" are correctly brought in and everybody is ready and waiting, one act before their one, in the back entrance. The orchestra strikes up the charivari and the clowns come tumbling into the ring.

Children, eyes shining, mouths agape, sit transfixed with anticipation as each act enters the ring - the acrobats with great energy and lithe bodies, leap, twist and somersault over the ground while the daring wire-walkers and flying trapeze artists perform their skills high overhead. The elephants lumber around the ring, liberty horses canter in file around the ring, the lady rider in her ballet costume of sequins and net, balances on the back of a white steed.

We must announce the interval, a short respite while the audience can buy ice cream, lemonade, candy floss etc. Whilst this is going on, we check to see that the lion cage is being put up correctly and safely so that the audience can admire the King of the Beasts as they stalk majestically around the cage.

The whistle is blown and the second half of the show continues. For another hour the audience is again lost in a fairytale world of lights and glittering spangles but all good things must come to an end - the anthem is played and the people file out of the big top, home to everyday life of ordinary normal existence the circus just a happy memory until next year when the big top returns to the common for its annual visit.

We however, have another show, the evening one, we must check everything again, snatch a hasty tea. Finally, the evening show is over, the last customer has left the menagerie where they have been watching the wild beasts being fed their supper, and this has to be done after the final performance. The animals do not like to work on full stomachs. We can then go and have our late-night supper before we tumble wearily into our beds to sleep, knowing that we have to go through the same routine again tomorrow before we move on to the next venue but happy knowing that we have done our job of entertaining the children and their parents for a couple of hours with "The Greatest Show on Earth."

If, however it is the last evening at the venue before they hit their beds, they have to take the big top down, fold and load on to the Lorries, along with the benches and chairs etc., feed and prepare the animals so that an early start can be made next morning. An early start is always required so they can get to the next venue with sufficient time to get the Big Top up, fit it out with the seating, platform and settle the animals down so they are ready for the afternoon performance. All members of the circus are involved, this also means the performers, male and females all mucking in, though in many cases the ladies will be preparing meals for their men folk, repairing costumes etc.

It is not unusual to recruit an army of small local boys to help out with some of the manual work. More often than not the circus would be performing at different venues every day, this means that the members including performing are working nothing less than a fourteen-hour day right through the circus season which normally starts around Easter time through to October.

Modern caravans have water and electricity but in the early days everything was moved from town to town in handcarts or horse drawn wagons. The traditional bow topped wagons looked romantic, but living in them was anything but – Joan explains 'We had to wash out in the open in a bucket, one foot in at a time. My mother used to be able to put a three-course meal on the table using a primus stove and if you had a gas lamp fitted you were really living it up.'

As Joan goes on to say: - 'It may be thrilling but it is hard work and during the season, nearly every engagement is a one-night stand. That is we visit a different town every day and when we arrive we all have to help to put up the King Pole, King Pole being the stout centre pole of the great circus tent normally referred to as Big Top.'

Circuses over time have evolved more so in the last few decades with the pressure of animal welfare at the forefront of the public minds and many of our travelling circuses today are animal free but there are still a few who use animal performances.

Although our Joan admires the talented artist circus performers, she was brought up with animals with horses being her favourite animal so to her a circus is not the same without its animals. She says that those involved with training wild animals should be referred to as animal trainers, not tamers. Wild animals such as lions can never become tame like cats and dogs, you can make friends of them but you'll never actually tame them.

Joan at the farm with her horses

The Opening Night

Excitement mounts as Lorries arrive
Their trailers with animals huddled inside.
Caravans park round the edge of the field,
We watch with wonder, our wide eyes peeled.

The Big Top is slowly hauled up high,
Its colourful canvases reach to the sky.
Sawdust is scattered inside the ring
And lights switched on to invite us in.

The brass band plays a rousing tune
As the ringmaster enters to cheers, and soon
The acrobats climb to the high trapeze
With gasps from the crowd as they swing with ease.

The sea lions honk and balance their ball
And clap their flippers to cheers from us all.
The fire-eater scares us with his daring feats,
As terrified children cling to their seats.

Six white horses with bobbing plumes
Trot round the ring to jaunty tunes,
Their bare-back riders perform with skill
Balancing acts to amaze and thrill.

The jugglers throw batons high in the air,
Then tumble and catch them with time to spare.
Laughter spreads as the clowns give chase,
Trip over each other and fall flat on their face.

The crack of a whip as the lions roar
And enter the ring with its sawdust floor.
They leap through hoops and rings of fire
Then jump over barriers higher and higher.

The band strikes up to end the show,
As amazed and delighted we homeward go.
Children with images filling their heads,
Happy to dream as they crawl into bed.
By Sue Ranford (Basildon Borough Heritage Society)

Chapter 3 - Circus Rosaire – Early Years

Ever since the early days, circuses throughout the World are mainly made up of families who can trace their descendants through generations of circus performers. Circus Rosaire is a typical case.

Built by Ted Bunning – Joan's father

When Fred Ross met and married his beloved Florence and started his tiny circus, even he, optimist though he must have been, could never have dreamed that the two of them would start a circus dynasty of performers, whose reputation would spread throughout the world and are still performing today, albeit in America. But what about Fred and Florence where did they come from and what made them start up a circus? Fred not surprisingly came from an old circus family on his mother's side and his father had worked on the fairgrounds. Fred became an accomplished clown, contortionist and stilt walker and when the opportunity arose, he would perform at various funfairs and music halls.

I feel however, it would be best for Fred himself to explain his early beginnings. The following is from the interview he gave to Charles Douglas-Brown in his article in the Essex Newsman – Friday 29 June 1945, while the circus was in Maldon, Essex.

'I was born in Saddleworth, on the Lancashire and Yorkshire border in 1877. I got a name at school for turning somersaults. When I left school, I began to take my natural agility more seriously. My uncle was Billy Ross, he was nine-stone-four and they said then he was a champion boxer.

The Count – 1932

Those were the days when folk in top hats laid wagers of fifty golden sovereigns on one fight. I was keen on boxing and acrobats and so were my two brothers, we used to try to copy our uncle's acts on the music halls. You know there were no cinemas then and the halls were in vogue. The three of us got to do things on the horizontal bars. My star piece was to jump on a scythe blade in my bare feet and cut two potatoes in doing it. Don't think I'm boasting but memories of those far off days are very dear to me. Our act made people of Oldham talk, that's where we went to when we moved from Saddleworth. We were engaged at the Gaiety Theatre in Oldham at four pounds a week between us and that was wealth in those days.

We were known as the "Ross Combination" and after the first week with the Gaiety Theatre we were offered and accepted a six-month engagement at £6. Then mother financed a small booth show for us. We got together a square show and went on tour, that's to say, a little fairground booth show, but we had differences, so I cleared off on my own and got work with a Mr Harrison who had his own square show round the fairs. It turned out that he did not have any money to pay me, so following an agreement I finished with him. We were in Lancaster at the time so I decided to go "busking" that is I was stilt-walking, clowning, jumping and doing anything that made a show. It did not last long and after a few weeks I got a job with Sedgwick's Menagerie. Their star turn was a lion-tamer who was called The Great Lorenzo. My job was to keep the audience amused while the lion cage was being erected. Lorenzo was a proper lion trainer and wore a uniform with gold lace and strappings. I left Sedgwick's after a year and went busking again, this time in Durham.

I met up with some chaps, times were low and we were giving stilt-walking performances in the streets. We were showing outside a hotel when I noticed an unusually pretty girl in the crowd. I was dressed and made up as a clown but I walked straight up to her and asked her if she would like to kiss me, her response was "What, kiss a face like that?" However, I was determined to see her again. It just happened that I had a bad toothache, so I made an excuse to ask my fair lady (Florence) what I should do about it.

Florence Arnold (Rosaire)

She suggested a glass of stout with a hot poker placed in it. She did this for me and believe it or not the cure worked. A month later we were married and worked together in music halls, with me whistling and Florence playing the piano. (Florence was in fact a widow when she met Fred).

I found out that her father owned several hotels and music halls and she got me a job in one of her father's halls for a time. We then decided to go off touring on our own. We were in a fairground in Manchester when we heard a terrific row between a man and his wife who ran a little square show. It turned out that their show wasn't paying, I strolled across and as I got there, he let go of one of the stays of the tent and it caved in. I took a terrific risk as the man was in a vile temper but I chanced butting in. "Don't do that old man," I said, "you can always sell your square show," "I'll sell," he yelled at me, "I'm sick of it," I offered £4, knowing it was worth a lot more but the man was in such a temper he did not realise what he was doing. I made sure I had a signed receipt before he changed his mind.

We opened up our own show which I pushed around in a handcart and painted the poles. I did a turn every half-hour and Florence stood out in front and managed the publicity side. It was rough on her as she was not used to the hard life of a fair ground but this was the beginning of our circus. We worked on the fairgrounds summer and winter and when we had our first baby, Aubrey, we rocked him to sleep in a swing-boat and as he slept we kept up my one man show with Florence standing outside the flare-lit booth contriving to attract the passer-by and so earn the three of us enough to live on. Eventually, we scraped together £15 for a top for a round tent. We stitched the walling ourselves and when we opened, we were a circus and not a square show any more. Everything we had in the world was in that tent and our little living-wagon which stood beside it. Our circus consisted at first of two ponies and ourselves, with occasional help from another man.

We had to think up acts which were within our limited resources and would appeal to the public. Florence would run one of the ponies round the ring and I'd say, "Now show us the girl who likes kissing in the dark!" Florence would pull the pony up somehow near one of the girls in our audience, it always caused a laugh. Then she would call on me to address the people and I'd say: Oh, I thought you said "Undress the people!" That sort of thing used to attract the people.

So, in a gradual way we built up our circus from a one-pole concern to the twenty lorry-loads it is today. Remember the sort of big-top tent we have here at Maldon costs approximately £400. I could if we had time to tell you story after story of the struggle to get our circus together and bring up eight children as well.'

It would have been around 1904 when Circus Rosaire came into being but unfortunately it is not known where the name came from though, we know there was a group calling themselves 'The Wondrous Rosaires' as early as 1891. They were performing in Manchester and a local advert read: -

THE WONDROUS ROSAIRES

(Four in Number), in their Marvellous Acrobatic Act and Triple Bar Artists, with Double Somersaults at Liberty Hall.'

The question is who the four were, was it Fred who would have only been 13 and his two younger brothers and their father? A year later they were at the Princes Theatre, Accrington before moving on to Liberty Hall:

THE ROSAIRES, Marvellous Gentlemen.

(The four smartest men the World has ever produced) Acrobats, Triple Bar Artists, with Double Somersaults and Comic Boxing Entree.

We find them again this time in Burnley in December 1899 (four of them) and in July 1900 at the Exeter races there was a horse called Rosaire running in the 2.30, odds 100 to 8. Question again was the horse named after the Rosaires or is it just a coincidence? They were still performing several years after Fred had supposedly started up his little circus, leading me to believe that they had no connection to Fred or his family but was it this group that inspired him to call his circus, 'Circus Rosaire?'

It was not long before they both became known as the 'Count' and 'Countess' and again it is unknown how this came about.

The Children – Second Generation

Fred and Florence had eight children, Aubrey (born 1904), Dennis (born 8 June 1908), Zena (born 5 October 1909),

Ivor (Born 1 July 1911), Cicily (born 28 October 1912), Vivienne (Born 1914), Derrick (Born 15 August 1916), Ida (born 16 April 1919). They all started performing at a very early age becoming talented performers, versatile as riders, clowns, acrobats, aerialist and animal trainers in their own right.

At first circus life was a struggle, there being considerable unrest in Europe that resulted in the First World War which did not help. All but one of the 'Count's' show horses were commandeered and he was consigned to work in a coal mine. Occasionally he would take some of the children down the mines. The young family after the war regrouped and during the interwar years the circus went from strength to strength.

This is what Rupert Croft-Cooke in his book 'The Happy Highways' had to say about the children: 'All the eight children had been brought up on the road and the clean outdoor and the vigorous routine they had followed from childhood had given each of them a splendid physique while the changes and chances of their life had inspired them with an alert, enquiring view of humanity, unreserved humour and an entirely amiable and natural vanity. Without having left England they were cosmopolitan. With little routine education they were sophisticated.'

Aubrey was born at the Ripponden fairground amongst the din of showman's drums and the music of the fair. He was destined to become one of the great clowns of the tenting circus. He was known as 'Jimmy Green' or 'Little Jimmy'. He was often assisted by his ring partners, Little Freddie and Charlie Austin, their gags, sketches and other comical entrees were always new and novel and their audiences were always kept amused with their merry antics.

He was adored and loved by the children. One report said 'Aubrey did not act the clown; the clown took possession of Aubrey.' He also performed on the rings and often to make a few extra pennies he participated in boxing matches in the fair's boxing booths and on one occasion ended up with a broken nose.

He married Helen Scotland in early 1937 who had also come from a large family of Scottish show-people. Unfortunately, unlike his brothers and sisters he died young on the 13 October 1941 while in Stirlingshire so he was never to see the golden years of the Rosaire Circus. He was buried in Aberlogie churchyard leaving behind not only his young wife but also baby daughter Denise.

Aubrey –Jimmy Green

Fool Moment

Clown, fool, it is me
A sparkling eye reveals in its deepness
Lies the uncovered smile.

Clown, fool, keep away
Say's uncontrollable vulnerability, I will
Be exposed

Clown, fool, reminds me
To forget self and let spontaneous
Laughter explode.

Awakening wisdom
As laughter's moment lifts the shadows
And finds my soul.

Unknown Author

'Jimmy Green' – 'Little Freddie' – 'Charlie Austin'

Dennis became one of the finest wire-walkers in the country, performing without a parasol often appearing in splendid Spanish costumes. This is not surprising as he married in 1939 Emilia (Amelia) Rubio who herself was a well-known Spanish acrobat and had appeared in America and in cabaret shows in several large hotels in London. They ran away together and got married without Amelia's parents' consent.

Dennis and Amelia had two children Carlos born in 1940 and Carmen born in 1941. Carmen like the rest of the Rosaire family was a talented trapeze artiste.

The local Billericay newspaper on 29 April 1955 reported on Rosaire Circus's first outing at the start of the Summer Touring Season at Sun Corner, Billericay:-

TRAPEZE THRILLS BY 15- YEAR-OLD BILLERICAY GIRL

'Thrills of the "Big Top" with its skilful horse riders, animal trainers and tumbling clowns and other laugh raising stunts were plentiful at Rosaire Circus at Billericay but the crowd reserved the biggest cheer for the youngest artiste of the company, 15-year-old Carmen Rosaire, for a breath-taking performance on the trapeze.

Although Carmen had been training for only a few months she had already mastered a number of daring acts. Also in the circus with her was her 16 year old brother Carlos performing on the trampoline and we must not forget their cousin, 20 year old Joan Rosaire an equestrian of great ability and charm and her wonder horse Goldy.'

Then in August 1960 disaster struck, Carmen while rehearsing her routine for a BBC TV show with Chipperfield's Circus her trapeze strap snapped, hurtling her to the sawdust ring. She was rushed to hospital where she died the following day. As you can imagine her family wept in particular her brother Carlos.

Two years later Carlos married Tina Paula at the Roman Catholic Church, Billericay. Tina was also a trapeze artist but she made a pact with her husband to be, that she would give up her job as a flying trapeze artist and instead do less dangerous circus work. Carlos's best man was 3ft. 6in. tall clown Alan Rosaire who was also his partner in a trampoline act. Alan surprisingly was no relation but we must remember that Carlo's name was Ross.

Tina had taken up trampolining and outside the church a day after her wedding and wearing a white lace crinoline gown she performed on the trampoline, no doubt with the intention of performing with her husband.

Dennis and the Countess – 1930s

Zena was the star on the rings, she was often joined by Ivor and Derrick but the rings were her speciality. She also performed on the high wire and did a contortionist act. Zena was however the least flamboyant of the Rosaires, but still contrived to do just about everything in the ring and was a tireless worker behind the scenes. During a winter lay-off she met and married Ted Bunning. Ted ran a garage and joinery business when he met Zena and proved to be a tremendous asset to the circus. The meeting came about following Aubrey taking a part of a lorry to be mended at the garage.

Ted and Zena wedding – Isle of Man 1931

Ted and Dennis Rosaire became a guiding force behind the circus following the death of the Count. They had the Count and Countess's first grandchild - our Joan - and he later built many of the splendid vehicles in which Joan and her horses lived and travelled together. Following the closure of the circus Zena and Ted returned to farming in Billericay. Zena died in 1974 but Joan remained at the family farm to look after her father until he died in 1985.

Ivor was born at Pontefract, Yorkshire he became a versatile acrobat, aerialist, bareback rider and barrel jumper. He also became one of the country's leading experts on elephant training and care. This came about when John Swallow joined Circus Rosaire in 1931 with the two famous veteran elephants, Salt and Sauce and Ivor was entrusted with their care.

Zena flying through the air

During the winter of 1938/39 Ivor along with his brother Derrick and Rupert Croft-Cooke in an old converted Morris Commercial van travelled around Europe including Germany and Austria. On his return the circus acquired its own elephant, Princess Monica, which Ivor trained and worked with the celebrated film star Sabu. He married Lucy Garner, a paper mill worker he met while the circus was appearing in Bowness, Bolton in 1939. They went on to have two children, Juliette and Derrick both of whom followed the family traditions and became talented circus artists. He served in the army from 1942 to 1946, when demobbed he re-joined the family circus, which had been playing in variety theatres during the winter months.

Chipperfield Circus was beginning to emerge as one of the largest travelling circuses in Britain and had around twenty elephants. Ivor was approached, and he went on to have an amazing career with the Chipperfields but also branching out and working for other circuses, as well as helping out with Circus Rosaire when at home and also in Europe. In one of his acts he had a fierce Bengal tiger riding on the back of a full-grown Asiatic elephant. He made a number of film appearances with Sabu and with Dirk Bogarde in Doctor in the House and in the T.V. show Double Your Money in which he won £250, while his elephant was presented with 250 currant buns.

Ivor with Princess Monica

When Lucy became sick and subsequently died in 1995 he retired to the farm in Billericay, where he died in December 2005 at the age of 94. He died in the same month as his brother Derrick.

Cicily, known as Cissy by Joan, was an all-round performer (rider, trapeze and general artiste) and elephant trainer. So, it is not surprising that when she married Walter Shufflebottom on 20 March 1937 at St Magdalen Church in Billericay High Street they arrived on two elephants. The elephants being none other than 'Salt and Saucy,' they left on one, I wonder which one? At one point one of them picked Cicily up by the head using its mouth. There was one scary moment when the elephants waiting outside the church became impatient and nearly caused a stampede as onlookers panicked. The event was photographed by the world-famous Pathe News. Not surprisingly it was also the day that Circus Rosaire had chosen to be their opening show of the season at Billericay. Our Joan was one of the bridesmaids.

They went on to have three children, Cicily Leonie, Walter and Roy. Leonie and Uncle Aubrey and Aunt Helen's daughter Denise of the same age were both christened at the church and as one would expect had their prams pushed to the church by elephants. Both events attracted enormous crowds a spectacle I doubt the town has experienced since.

Walter came from a circus background where the main theme was based on the Wild West. He was an accomplished knife-thrower and whip-cracker. He teamed up with Cicily and they worked the various fair grounds in a Western show where she would stand at a special wooden board whilst Wally as he was known used her as a target to throw knives and hatchets at. As you can imagine it was a very exciting display which the audience loved and as Joan said, 'I as usual hoped that one day I could take Aunt Cissy place, which in due course did happen.'

There is no doubt that on occasions they performed the act for Circus Rosaire, in fact they teamed up with Derrick Rosaire to form 'Shufflebottoms Circus' in 1946 and 1947. Wally was one of the last showmen to present a live Western Show on British fairgrounds in the 1960s.

Joan explains: - 'Walter's father William a Yorkshireman went to America with his Wild West Act and it appears he met up with Buffalo Bill's show, returning to England with his circus "Rifle Bill's Wild West".'

Unfortunately, in 1916 he suffered a fatal accident. He had been riding a horse which was being lassoed by another performer. The lasso got caught up round the horse's legs and pulled it down; William fell to the ground breaking his neck.

Wally and the family decided to stay in England and in addition to him being a knife thrower he was also an excellent sharp

shooter. One trick in particular was very exciting; he used to shoot the bowl of a pipe from Aunt Cissie's nose.

Cicily and Walters Wedding

. Wally made the pipes himself from pitch and as the pitch was black, he used to dip the pipes in white wash. When they performed Cissy used to cover her face with a handkerchief so that nothing got in her eyes. When Leonie was old enough, she used to perform all the parts her mother did and as she got older learned to shoot as well. One trick she performed was to shoot a pipe off the target's nose whilst leaning over backwards. As far as Joan is aware, she was the only girl who could perform this trick.'

Vivienne was born in Hemsworth, Yorkshire and like her siblings was a talented circus performer her speciality being the trapeze and she often performed with her sister Ida and Brother Dennis. Her ring name was 'La Petite Vivienne.'

Vivienne met James O'Brien who was also from a family of travelling showmen. They married in Whitchurch, Shropshire in 1942 but James spent a good part of the Second World War abroad, serving as a Sergeant. Their wedding ceremony was quite a spectacle, which included snakes, elephants and tigers as guests along with a military sword salute from James's army friends. Three children followed, James, and twin daughters Alison and Vivienne.

After 30 odd years travelling around the various fairgrounds they decided to settle down in Arbroath, Scotland and open up a cover fair, they named it Pleasure Land. It is still run by the family and is believed to be the largest indoor funfair in Tayside and Angus with games, rides, and slot machines with the sounds and smells of a traditional Fairground.

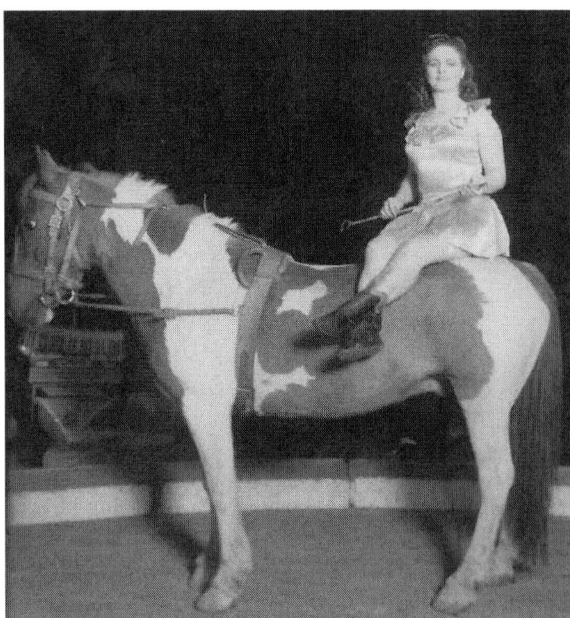

Vivienne on Duke – 1944

Derrick was born as the Battle of Verdun was being raged during the First World War and was subsequently christened Derrick Verdun. The Battle of Verdun had commenced on the 21st February 1916 and raged until the 18th December 1916 the longest battle of the war fought between the French and Germans. While this was going on the British were fighting their own battle against the Germans on the Somme.

Derrick at times could be a bit of a devil, he had a habit of jumping over the horses as they were pulling the various carts and on one occasion he fell over and the cart ran over him damaging his back and spine. The doctors did not think he would walk again but he proved them wrong and he went on to become an excellent performer. He also developed his own sideshow featuring a variety of exotic animals which included a bear, leopard and lion which gave him the idea later in life of forming his own zoo.

Derrick

Derrick served in the Army during the Second World War but found time to marry Betty Kayes on 14 June 1943 in Blackpool. Betty was also from a well-known circus family. They were to have five children, Elaine, Pamela, Linda, Kay and Derrick Jnr and like all the other grandchildren they became talented circus performers.

After the war Derrick and Betty did not return to the family circus but branched out on their own with a horse act and Pekingese dogs working in other circuses and in variety and music halls although they did return when there was no work elsewhere. Derrick continued to develop his horse act with his horse 'Tony' and it became a very popular feature in variety. He followed the popular American film star Roy Rogers and Trigger at the London Palladium achieving higher acclaim from the critics than his better-known rival. He toured extensively in Europe with various circuses.

Derrick and Betty with their Pekingese dogs

Our Joan by watching Derrick's act developed a similar act with her horse 'Goldy' and when Tony fell sick, she would loan Goldy to him to be able to continue his work in Europe. In turn, he passed to her a contract with the Spanish Circo Americano, while he worked at Circo Prince, a situation which frequently led to them appearing in big tops together at fiestas. They also appeared in 1958 with the Swiss National Circus Knie. Derrick presented Tony, Joan rode in a Western display and his little daughter Linda presented the Pekingese dog act.

In 1960 Derrick and his family went to America to appear on the 'Ed Sullivan Show.' They soon became involved in many of the leading circuses etc. Eventually he established his own zoo in Pennsylvania and at one time was the owner of a huge brown bear that featured in the popular television series Grizzly Adams.

The family never returned to their native roots in England. Betty died in 1983, he later remarried to Liza Hernandez a former Mexican circus acrobat. Derrick as already mentioned passed away in December 2005 the same month and year as his brother Ivor. The family however is still going strong in America with each of the children actively involved with animals in some form or another and are constantly in touch with Joan.

Ida was the last of the children, being born just after the end of the First World War. She became an accomplished voltige rider, stage name 'Ida Zanetta'. She also worked as an acrobat and performed in flying trapeze acts as already mentioned with her sister Vivienne and brother Dennis. Her most daring act was allowing Saucy the elephant to carry her around the ring in his mouth.

Her first husband Martin Russell Hawkes who she married in 1939 in Sevenoaks, Kent was a son of a vicar from Sevenoaks. He joined the circus with his gang of trained poodles. He later graduated to training the circus lions. He gave Ida a gift of a pure white Pekingese which became the star of her act when she took over from Martin. She also appeared in other circuses and variety shows with the act. They later divorced and Ida remarried Sam Smith, a Londoner who ran a coal yard, where many circuses and fairground folk often wintered.

Ida's last show appearance for Circus Rosaire was in the summer of 1954. She died on 24 July 2011 in Reading at the age of 92. Her son David took over her act, starring in circuses around the world and is still performing in the United States.

Ida on Duke

The farm, 'Wilborough' Cox's Farm Road, Billericay was acquired by Fred in the early 1930s and it became the circus winter home. From then on it resulted in their first performance of a new circus season being performed at Sun Corner, Billericay.

The whole family would descend on the farm but would continue to live in their caravans. If they could not find work performing in various theatres around the country, they would look for local temporary jobs. Joy Springate who lived locally in Billericay during the sixties and seventies remembers that Derek

Owles who had married Cicily Leonie and that Cicily used to work at the local Ball Plastics factory every winter.

Joy worked for a local supermarket, 'Robinson' and remembers frequently serving Cicily and that her son Graham regularly played with Cicily's son Paul, both being of the same age.

The Rosaire Family 1931

The circus during the interwar years received many an accolade: -

Cornishman 22 July 1937.

'Rosaire's British and Continental Circus which arrived at Penzance on Sunday, fulfilled a two days engagement at the Recreation Ground on Monday and Tuesday. This circus embraces everything the public look forward to seeing in this particular line - performing elephants, horses, ponies, dogs, monkeys etc., which pleased lovers of animals - and the latest sensations. These include The Bales, the world's greatest trick cyclists looping the loop on the back of a motor cycle and flying trapeze, aerial bar and trampoline performers.'

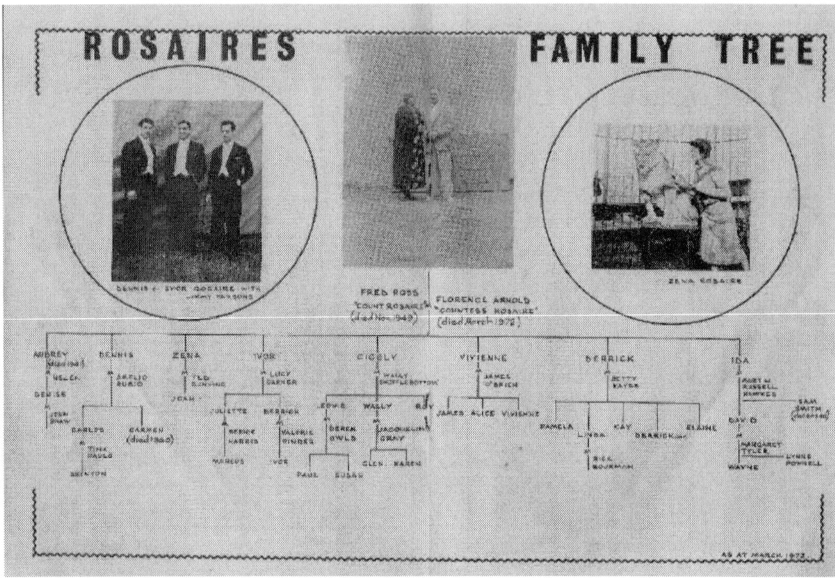

Rosaire Family Tree as at March 1973 – (King Pole Magazine April 1973)

Daily Mirror 22 November 1938 – 'Swing Time on the Farm'

'Swinging calmly from a trapeze, they performed hair-raising acrobatics while the other family members looked on; awaiting their turn and that goes for the little girl too.

For these are all members of the Rosaire family, famous circus folk and expert trapeze and trick-riding artists, every one of them. Here you see Ida and Vivian Rosaire rehearsing for the Christmas season down on the farm in Billericay, Essex.' It's no doubt that little girl was our Joan!

There were however on occasions a few unexpected, scary and tragic moments. For example, in August 1931 while the circus was appearing at Ramsey, Isle of Man, Ivor who was performing nightly with his sister on a trapeze bar found himself having to dash into the sea where she had got into difficulty and save her from drowning.

Then the Nottingham Journal in October 1938 reports the tragic death of one of its assistant elephant keepers. Aubrey told the reporter that at about one o'clock that afternoon he heard a shout from the elephants tent and running in he found William Aslett, who had been recently taken on as an assistant to the elephant keeper lying on his back with his ribs terribly crushed. It is believed that a tent peg had been drawn out and part of the tent had sagged inwards. The elephant appeared to have moved forward drawing out the tent peg and Aslett who must have tried to replace it, fell on his back and he was accidently crushed by the elephant's foot. His last words were 'He's finished me this time.' When the accident happened the elephant, called Salt was soon to enter the ring for an afternoon performance, in which it carried in Ida with her head in its mouth. Verdict - Accidental death.

Then in November 1938 with the circus back at its winter quarters in Billericay a red soldier monkey escaped from its cage and was at large for three days before it was recaptured. Mrs Cottingham of Westholme, West Hanningfield, discovered the monkey in her bungalow. She shut it in and obtained assistance of a neighbour. After considerable difficulty it was enticed into a chicken crate with a banana as bait. It was found that the monkey had raided the larder and eaten a number of cakes. It was taken to Chelmsford Police Station and later claimed by Circus Rosaire.

Jumping forward for a moment to December 1942 we have the Yorkshire Evening Post reporting on one of Rosaire's lions escaping:-'During a performance by Rosaire's Circus at Nottingham Empire last night (Friday 18th), Leo, a lion, escaped from the cage, ran off the stage and made for another cage containing a lioness and a cub, of which he is the father. The safety curtain was lowered, all doors leading to the stage were locked and the audience told the show was over. Leo was induced back into the cage by his trainer, the circus staff and stage hands, with a piece of horse meat as bait.

On the road - and is that our Joan on the horse in front - late 1930s

In August 1946 we find that another pet monkey, belonging to a member of the circus escaped while the circus was visiting Whitstable. The monkey was allowed the freedom of the circus and was apparently attracted by the fruit trees in the gardens adjoining the Recreation Ground. Circus hands and residents attempted for some time to catch it but as they drew near, the animal obviously enjoying new-found freedom, jumped over the fences from garden to garden, leaving its baffled pursuers far behind. Eventually the chase was given up and the monkey was left to its own devices. A few days later it allowed a little girl living in nearby Railway Avenue to pick it up and she immediately returned it to the grateful owner. A brave little girl, not sure I would have picked it up.

In July 1947 Salt and Sauce and another elephant were up to their tricks again. This time the Ringland Circus was parked up at Shortwood Common, Staines, Middlesex. A dairymaid, Brenda Gray was sitting at her home at Shortwood Farm when she suddenly heard a crashing of glass, she ran outside to see what was happening and came face to face with three elephants. One had pushed its trunk through a glass window of the cow shed and the others were trying to smash the farm gate. Brenda grabbed a pitchfork to fend off the elephants and managed to barricade the farm gate and checking to see her mother was locked in the kitchen, ran off across the farm to get help from the circus.

Ivor Rosaire appeared and the elephants calmly returned to the field the circus had rented. The manager of the circus apologised but explained the elephants could smell the cattle food in the cowshed. He also explained that they had rented the field and were allowed to let elephants stroll about to eat the grass. They always look out for any houses but missed this one because it was tucked away in the corner of the field.

On Saturday 20th February 1954 during a matinee given by the circus at Aston Hippodrome a lion clawed one of the circus trainers in the last act of the show. The trainer left the stage and the curtain came down without the audience realising that anything untoward had happened. During the bathing of the trainer's hand the musical director had his hand bitten by a lioness as he attempted to take a bottle of disinfectant from the top of her cage. The injuries were not that serious and though both men attended Birmingham General Hospital, they were soon back at the theatre.

Not good reading but considering the number of circuses across the world and the number of shows performed every year for the past 200 years or more it's not surprising that a few accidents occur.

Salt and Sauce.

Mention has been made on several occasions about this pair of famous Indian elephants so I believe a little more background information is required. They were both born in 1900, brought over to England by Carl Hagenbeck a German animal trainer and agent who sold them to George William Lockhart and over the next fifty odd years were owned and presented by some of the most famous show business people of their era.

John Swallow, owner of Bronco Bill's Circus acquired them in the early 1920s, then in 1931 joined the Rosaire Circus and Ivor Rosaire took over their care. He went on to train them to play cricket and football and he believed that one of the successes of the Rosaire show was the appeal of the elephants.

Another of their tricks was to stand on two legs, squat on their vast haunches and one of them to the delight and alarm of the audience, carried Ivor's sister Ida around the ring in their mouth. A year later both Salt and Sauce appeared in the film 'Elephant Boy',

I wonder, is this our Joan with Salt and Sauce

Though they became famous for their vast array of tricks, unfortunately they were also feared for their temperamental moods. Sauce often referred to as 'Saucy' had been involved in the death of George William Lockhart in 1904 when he was crushed during a stampede at Walthamstow Station and Salt killed as already described William Aslett in 1938.

John Swallow died in 1945 and his wife and their son donated them to Dudley Zoo to commemorate his memory. They were happy knowing that they would have a good home and in return would give pleasure to children for years to come. That knowledge would have made their father very happy.

Unfortunately, they were very difficult to handle so a year later Tom Fossett acquired them for his circus 'Fossett's Ringland's Circus' with Ivor in charge again. Ivor in fact had just come back from five years in the army as a Sergeant Instructor. The elephants went mad with excitement when they saw him.

In 1952 Salt accidentally got stuck in Vauxhall Lake while touring with the Ringland's circus. It took seven hours with the aid of a crane before they could free her. Unfortunately, she suffered from pneumonia and died a week later. Sauce died of natural causes in 1960.

Our Elephants

The *elephants lumber into the ring*
To the sound of the band echoing
A sombre tune to the elephants' gait
As with baited breath we wait.

Trunks curled round the tail in front
They're ready to perform amazing stunts,
They wait, sentinel, on a tiny stand,
Their feet together, as the band
Begins to play a jaunty theme
That signals the start of their circus routine.

Their snake-like trunks wave high in the air
Conducting the band with an elegant flair.
We watch as the trainer's whistle blows
And the elephants adopt an impressive pose.
They reach up high as if to beg
Balancing on their huge hind legs.

They dance a little conga hop,
Turn in a circle, and slowly stop.
These towering giants leave the ring
To the sound of clapping and loud cheering.
They stare with a liquid, doleful eye,
Wink at the crowd to say, "Goodbye."

By Sue Ranford (Basildon Borough Heritage Society)

Little Freddy, Zena, Ivor, Aubrey and Salt and Sauce

Before moving on with Joan and the rest of the Rosaires story, I feel it is worth mentioning that around the turn of 1900 another circus was trying to establish its winter quarters at North Benfleet only a few miles away from where the Rosaires were later going to set up.

A circus owner from Europe by the name of Mr Dainz decided to come to England and try his luck. A theatre manager thought an animal show might fill some seats, so he hired Mr Dainz who had very large and clever dogs and goats and at the first show he put on, an attendant noticed a rumple in the stage carpet so he went on carefully facing the audience and bent forward to pull the carpet into place. For the waiting goats this was too great a temptation and one hustled forward and butted him from behind, sending the poor man head on into the orchestra pit. The applause was thunderous and the theatre was packed for a week waiting for the goats to perform again but of course they didn't, but Dainz circus had arrived. The star of the show however was not the goats but a very clever donkey called 'Smiler.'

At the end of his first season he needed somewhere to keep his animals during the winter. He found a farm in North Benfleet up for sale called Coblows or Cold Blows. He bought it and renamed it after his donkey 'Smilers Farm' and the name still survives to this day.

Two of his southernmost fields would flood during the winter so he decided to sell them off as building plots. The Plotland era had reached North Benfleet. Being of foreign origin he had a fascination for the English royalty so he named two of the roads he had laid out, Osborne Road and Windsor Road. Unfortunately, we know very little about his circus and what happened to it.

Chapter 4 - Circus Rosaire – 1940/1950s

Front Row-left to right – David, Carlos, Carmen, Julliet
Second Row – Left to right – Ivor, Count, Countess, Butch Reynolds, Little Harold, Jim Zola
Back Row – Dog, Paddy, Babs Zola, Joan?
Photo Mid/late 1940s

During the interwar years the circus as indicated was going from strength to strength. Unfortunately, the Second World War intervened and most of the circus men went off to fight, leaving the women folk to make sure that the shows continued to entertain the public. One of the many problems though, was that you could not use lights at night. To overcome this Joan's father made masks out of old saucepans to go over the lights. Petrol was also a problem as it was on coupons, this was probably one of the reasons why circuses started staying in one place for more than one day. It was during this period though, that more women started to drive the Lorries. It also meant the performing horses had to be harnessed up to pull the wagons from town to town. The food situation for the animals was also very difficult, also, the other problem was that all the road signs had been taken down so they marked the roads with sods of earth for those that were following but somehow, they managed.

Joan believed it was vitally important that they help keep the morale of the people up. It was during this period that they became one of Britain's best medium-size travelling circuses.

From 1941 to 1943 they teamed up with Sidney Burns and Regis productions. The arrangement was terminated on the 10th April 1943 and Regis Productions made the following announcement. 'Thanks to Mr and Mrs Fred Rosaire, artists and staff for their co-operation in making the last two years tour the Biggest War-Time success in show business.'

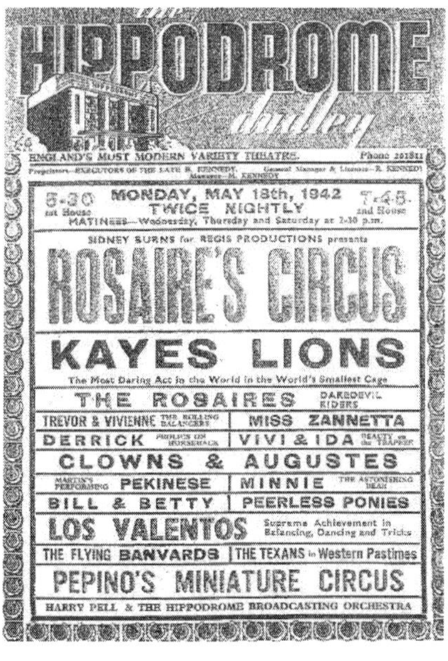

In 1942 was possibly Circus Rosaire and the whole family's finest hour. King Peter of Yugoslavia along with his sister and King George of Greece attended a special Royal

Command performance by the circus on Hampstead Heath with top comic Tommy Trinder immaculately attired acting as the ringmaster. The performance was in aid of the 'Yugoslavia Relief Fund,' it helped establish the circus as one of the top circuses in the land. King George declined to occupy the Royal Box, saying he preferred an ordinary ringside seat, presumably he wanted to soak up the circus atmosphere. Also in attendance was Princess Romanovsky-Pavlovsky who was the chairwoman of the committee of the Yugoslavia Relief Fund. The Princess before her marriage to Prince Vsevolod Ivanovich of Russia was Lady Mary Lygon, daughter of the Earl and Countess Beauchamp.

Thousands of circus fans mobbed the 'Big Top' and the tent was packed, unfortunately there were as many fans left outside as in. If the tent was twice the size it would still have not got everybody in. It turned out to be a great show with the majority of the Rosaire family joining in, even Ivor Rosaire was given special leave from the army in order to render assistance.

Princess Pavlovski, King Peter and King George

Joan, though only nine at the time remembers the occasion well, 'I particularly remember a conversation King George was having with Grandfather.' He said 'I believe sir you are known as the Count. Oh yes sir but that is just a bit of circus fun. King Peter then said to Grandfather, Well sir I shall bestow this title upon you and henceforth you shall be known as Count Rosaire and madam Rosaire as Countess.'

Royal Command Show – Yugoslavia War Fund

A couple of weeks later though just before the circus was due to open at the Bristol Empire the police banned Tommy Kayes and his Lions appearing on the show in the interest of public safety. As you can imagine the uproar it caused, considering the act had been shown all over the country and a few weeks earlier in front of Royalty. The ban had been brought about by the fact that a boy had recently been mauled to death by a lioness but as Joan had previously said, considering this and the terrible war it was important to keep the morale of the people up. There is no doubt that Circus Rosaire played their part and the following is a report in the **'The Scotsman' – Tuesday 14 April 1942:-**

'Seats were at a premium for the opening performance of Rosaire Circus at the Empire Theatre, Edinburgh last night. Eager shouts when the ponies pranced into the ring, shrill laughter at the antics of the clowns and tense excitement when one of the lions was crashing against the bars of the cage before the trainer found the right moment to step inside were among the signs of the appreciative children in the audience, who were perhaps receiving a special indulgence during the school holiday period. It was apparent however that they required the attendance of many who, in heart to enjoy the familiar thrills and unsophisticated pleasure of the "big top," and they were not disappointed in their expectations of two hours' diversion from war-time cares. It was surprisingly good stage substitute for the attractions of the circus in its usual spacious setting under canvas. The members of the Rosaire family helped to keep the show going at a fast pace and were aided by talented colleagues and animal performers. There were ponies which raced round the ring with daring riders, or did tricks with uncanny deliberation, a Pekinese dog with a gift for "hurdling," a bear (Minnie) which came on with ungainly intentness for its "rations," roller balancers, graceful trapeze and tight-wire performers, a knife thrower whose dexterity made young folks gasp. Pepino' circus in miniature, with ponies, dogs and a monkey which rode tenaciously on the back of one of the dogs and the culminating thrill provided by Tommy Kayes and his lions.'

In September 1944 the circus was visiting Wrexham and the local paper had this to say about the circus and our Joan: -

'This well-known circus visited the lovely park of Wrexham for three days on Monday, Tuesday and Wednesday of last week and performed to packed houses for the three days. The show is beautifully clean and is painted in red, white and blue. Little Joan, a second generation of Rosaire's family, is eleven years of age and is remarkably clever in each act.'

1943 – Left to Right – Children – Carmen, Carlos, David, Joan – Adults – Amelia, Dennis, Count, Countess, Vivienne, Ida, Zena.

Margaret Stanbury reported on the Billericay Community Archive website that as a child during WW2, she lived in Billericay Police Station which was across the road from the field at Sun Corner upon which the Circus used to perform. There were garages at the rear with an outside tap and they used to bring the elephants over and hose them down and scrub them with a yard broom. 'As a small child this was fascinating and the circus is something I will never forget.'

After the war the circus gathered pace again and this is what Rupert Croft-Cooke had to say in 1948: -

‘It will be good news to all lovers of the true circus that the Rosaire Brothers are taking their grand family show out again this year. Dennis Rosaire has just returned from an enormously successful tour of Spain where the circus artist had terrific competition against the Torero (bullfighter) and had actually fought with them. Ivor after his war service as a P.T. Instructor, returns to the family a better performer than ever. And the boys have collected some first rate talent for this season regarding the Rosaire family as something of a miracle – father, mother, sons and daughters are all great artists. Now that they are getting together for the tenting season it will mean thrills for many thousands of children and adults in whatever part of England they visit.’

Joan on the bottom Step – Count and Countess on the top step – Chester 1945

Another reporter had this to say about our Joan: 'I have been more than pleased to see over the last two years some very promising young people. To this list of teenies one may safely add Joan. There is nothing precocious about her; she has a nice manner and ring style. Neither childish nor affecting, she is sophisticated but her personality for her age is rightly balanced. She is nicely and naturally spoken and above all, she shows a quiet confidence in what she has to do. This is particularly noticeable in her presentation of a trick horse and also when immediately after, she is seen and heard handling a charge vastly different – the comedy horse. In giving this little lady an encouraging pat on the back, one must also say "thank you" to her parents.' ....What a reference!

The King Pole December 1992 magazine under the article entitled: 'The Raw Real Stuff' (Tenting circuses in Wales of the forties and fifties) we find the following report on the Rosaires.

'Another show to call on us – in 1947 – was Rosaire's formerly "All British" but by now "British and Continental" Circus. Hal Thomas described in a letter to the magazine how, travelling with the show that year what he remembered. The show was presided over by the likeable, sanguine Count Fred Rosaire…but it was the formidable Countess who controlled the business. The children were whole-hearted performers in the ring and very versatile – riding, tumbling, flying rings, trampoline, triple bars etc', each trying to outdo the others.'

Thomas also recollects seeing Derrick Rosaire's pekes in 1947 when they featured in Wally Shufflebottom's Texan Wild West Circus. This show, starring the proprietor, with, notably, his knife throwing number, usually played in the fairgrounds but had been expanded into a fully-fledged circus only for this season.

Useful reinforcement came from animal members owned or trained by Derrick Rosaire (whose sister Cissy was Mrs Shufflebottom), among them a comedy black bear, Tony the golden horse of the West and some liberty horses.

One of the circus's and Joan's most terrifying moments was in 1948 when the circus was in Jersey and a gale blew the tents down but more on this later.

Circus Company getting ready to fly to Jersey 1948

Zena, Charlie Beckett, Dennis and Emelia – Jersey 1948

In 1949, the show was back in Aberystwyth, minus one or two family members and re-titled Rosaire Bros. Circus. On the all-the-acts poster were: - 'Leon, charming and sweet ballerina on horseback; the Ladderites on the breakaway ladder; the Poponoffs on the trampoline; the Zanettas, (Zena) flying rings; and Bong-Bongo-Bongo – he's left the Congo – with performing goat and monkeys. Top billing was shared by Los Valentos (Dennis Rosaire), the Spanish wizard on the wire and Ida Rosaire's Pekin Dogs, a delightful act reminiscent of that created by her brother Derrick and presented by his wife Betty, the non-riding member of the Kayes family.'

Countess, Zena and little Joan

In March 1949, Janice Farmer a journalist on the Essex Chronical paid the circus a visit at Billericay: -

‘In a large field in Cox’s Farm Lane there is a great deal of excitement as the Rosaire Circus prepares for the opening of the tenting season. I was met at the gate by a large white llama which ambled playfully towards me. Among the other animals were monkeys, horses, ponies, Pekinese dogs, lions, rabbits, guinea pigs, a bear and a goat.

Ivor Rosaire for example was in Sweden at the time of my visit presenting elephants in a circus there. Joan in fact can carry out her act with Goldy, in French, German and Swiss. Dennis the elder brother acts as general manager. He performs a wire-walking act in the show but has had several different jobs during his career. In 1946 he was bullfighting in Spain.

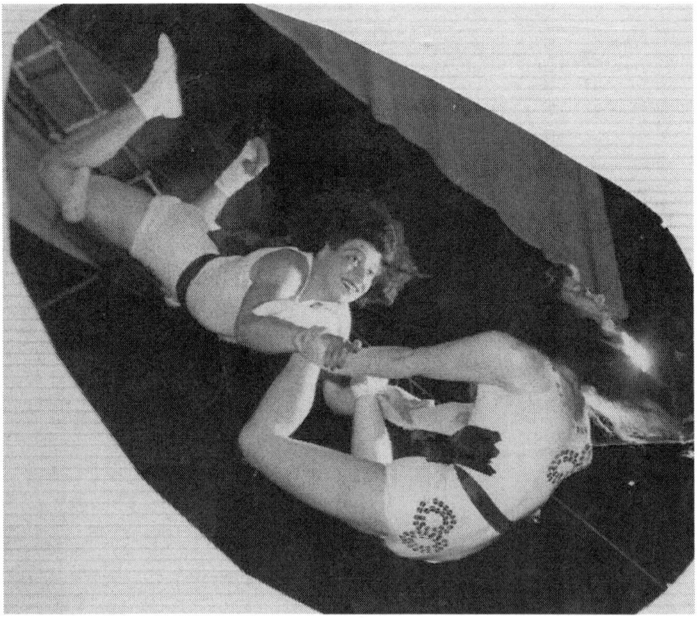

Joan and mother Zena on the rings and trapeze in Manchester

Zena Rosaire was sharpening up her trapeze act and with her was Joan her 16 year old daughter the circus ballerina of the show and who also presents the horses and ponies which she trains herself. She is passionately fond of horses and has won several prizes in show jumping. Ida Rosaire was also there getting ready and as the rest of the family says, "has an uncanny way with dogs." She trains twelve little Pekinese dogs in addition she also performs a trapeze and voltige act.

The rest of the family were gradually returning to the fold in time for the tenting season but we must not forget the background staff who build the vans and seats for the circus when required and designed and made the costumes and harness, apart from doing the skilled jobs such as electric welding. They are all closely watched over by their ever-vigilant parents – Count and Countess.'

Unfortunately, the Count died eight months later at Wilboughby Farm on 9 November 1949 from cancer. Rupert Croft-Cooke and Peter Cotes said in their book 'Circus' that he was a man of great courage, firm as a rock, with intense but quiet feelings, he was kind, generous and always loyal to his friends.

Florence died in 1972 at the age of 94, at her home 'Melbourne' next to the farm in Billericay. She was buried next to her Count at Brentwood Cemetery. Rupert Croft-Cooke in his book 'The Happy Highways' had this to say about her: - 'Her life had been spent in the living-waggons, moving over the country without more than a winter's rest. Yet she had a culture, a knowledge of men and things, a sense of proportion and criticism, out of keeping with her origins.'

It is obvious that from the humblest of beginnings they succeeded in establishing one of the finest tenting circuses in England and they trained all their children to become supreme circus artists and subsequently they trained their children to follow in their footsteps.

Following the death of the Count, the running of the circus fell to Ted (Bunning) and Zena, Joan's parents and Dennis Rosaire.

It is very difficult to decide which era was the circus's greatest period, was it the inter-war years or after the Second World War up to the mid -1950s, so it is a little surprising that the circus closed down around the end of 1956 even though they were still receiving glowing reports, along with our Joan.

The 'Counts' last photograph
Back Row – Martin Hawkes, Ted Bunning, Zena, Charlie, Emelia, Dennis, Joan
Middle Row- Viv, Countess, Count, Cissy
Front Row – Ida, Arthur Grice, Carlos

. The following are just a few as they travelled around the country: -

1949 – Billericay – Circus is coming to Town

'Rosaire grandchildren will take a bow – When Billericay's own circus – Rosaire Bros. – takes to the road again in two weeks' time the four children especially will be overjoyed. These four are the third generation of the Rosaire family in the circus and through the winter at Wilboughy Farm, Billericay they have been secretly practising acts of their own.

The Rosaires – father and mother both aged 73 four daughters and their husbands, four sons and their wives and 12 grandchildren – have "wintered" their circus in Billercay for 15 years. They chose the town because of its "healthy atmosphere" and beautiful countryside and now the thought of "wintering" anywhere else is just not entertained.

All twelve children are experienced travellers and consequently linguists of some distinction. The four who hope to take an active part this season are Joan (16), Carlos (9), David (9) and Carmen (7). One day they hope to achieve fame as their grandfather did. He was "every-thing" in the circus – trapeze, clown and acrobatics, were among his acts. His wife looked after the business side. Both are retired now but remain with the circus wherever it goes.

New acts are being prepared for this season and up-to-date equipment is being put together. A "royal" spot on the bills will be prepared for a recent acquisition – 12 trained Pekingese dogs. Another turn will be the monkey and the goat, who have endeared themselves to the children.

The show opens in Billericay on April 1 for two days only, then it moves to Laindon, Wickford and Vange, before going on tour in North Wales.'

The Laindon location was possibly behind the Laindon Hotel where many fairs, school races, football matches etc. were held.

1949 – Aylesbury, Buckinghamshire

Again, in his book 'The Circus has no Home' Rupert Croft-Cooke wrote of Joan 'at five years old her tiny legs in jodhpurs she would balance herself on the back of a white pony'. 'Well it is this same young lady at sixteen who has a particular talent in regards to horses and ponies and her trick riding shows great promise although she only embarked on this type of equestrianism at the start of the year.'

He continued 'Joan looking very neat in brown breeches, white boots, white shirt-blouse and with hair in two pigtails, showed no lack of assurance as she puts two horses through liberty evolutions, followed by a single horse (no doubt Goldy) in such items of sketch – lie-down and kiss –rumba-conversation-back out and then return to push her out, but she was soon back to present the pony Joey. This was all after Joan had helped to present the voltige where Joan picks the hankie up.'

1950 – Chessington

'Joan daughter of Zena and Ted Bunning was responsible for presentation of "Rosaire Liberty Horses" and right well did she do it too. She is still quite young to be entrusted with this sort of self-possession while her personality proved vastly pleasing.

Joan and Goldy at Chessington

Furthermore, it was evident that in her circus upbringing attention had been paid to that vital matter of deportment. As for the horses and ponies, their quality should have satisfied the most exacting, well trained and very well-conditioned.'

1950- Scunthorpe – Lincolnshire

'One item which attracted very considerable attention was the presentation by Miss Joan Rosaire of Rosaire's Liberty Horses and "Monty" the almost human pony; at seventeen years I consider this graceful performer a star.'

1950-Chelmsford

The circus opened for two days in April and Joan as it was now becoming a habit received very good reviews – featuring those two very versatile youngsters, Joan and Arthur the article goes on to say – 'Joan Rosaire promises well, not only for her bareback riding and ballerina but also for her handling of the Liberty horses.'

The Stage – Llandudno 12 July 1951

'Something entirely new in summer entertainment in the town is at the Grand, where Rosaire Circus is appearing. This circus is owned and managed by the Rosaire family and there are few circus lovers ignorant of its existence. The most sensational act is that of Los Miras, daring and accomplished Spanish aerial acts. Beauty on the trapeze is the contribution of Victoria and Los Valentinos depicting Spanish rhapsody on the high wire. The Arturos are impressive on the trampoline and Charles and Partner raise many laughs with their clowning.

Apollo the Scottish Samson is as strong as he looks and the Vera Valentine troupe of acrobats, newly arrived from Paris, are clever. Charlie Bale gives an impression of Charlie Chaplin and the Dareskas prove masters of bareback riding. Also in the circus are the Flying Rosaires (trapezists) and Joan Rosaire, a horseback ballerina. Jim Parsons introduces his African lions and the circus also possesses a trained llama and performing geese. The circus orchestra is under the direction of Cecil Rhodes.'

Circuses at Chessington Zoo (1951/52)

Chessington Zoo for the first time decided to book a complete circus for the Easter Holidays. The circus booked was none other than Circus Rosaire who provided the following acts:

- Los Valentos, the Spanish themed low wire act of Dennis Rosaire assisted by his wife Amelia.
- The Arturos trampoline act featuring Dennis in clown makeup along with his wife and son Arthur.
- Dennis was also involved in the Flying Rings, again as the clown but this time working with sister Zena and son Arthur.
- Joan with the liberty horses.
- Along with Arthur, Joan contributed a voltige act dressed as a Cossack.
- Ida with her troupe of Pekinese dogs.
- Roller balancing by Charlie Bale assisted by his mother Meta.
- The Chessington elephant Comet presented by Jim Parsons, the ringmaster.

Jim Parsons and his African Lions

Joan with Betsy a Grey getting ready for a performance somewhere in Devon - 1952 - Joan explains that whenever there was a break in performance she would go down onto the beach and collect winkles and cockles, in fact anything that was eatable and bring them back for mother to cook.

- Clowning was provided by Dennis and Charlie Bale dressed as Charlie Chaplin. Dennis also put a squad of geese through their paces.

Circus Rosaire was in great demand and had other commitments including a resident season at Bridlington and so they departed at the end of the Easter fortnight.

However, the show was obviously a success because they were invited back for the Easter show the following year and also for the summer season. The show this time comprised of the following acts:

- Voltige by Joan
- Clown Billy Howard with a llama
- Roller balancing by Charlie Bale. The final trick saw him balancing from his mouth a structure surmounted by a

starry, flag topped globe from which projected three arms each carrying a miniature aeroplane. As he descended the steps from the pedestal the globe and planes spun round.

- Three geese drilled by the ringmaster Jim Parsons. The geese waddled round the ring, balanced on a seesaw, slid down a chute and avoided jumping a bar.
- Joan with two grey horses followed by a pony with a dog as a jockey.
- Charlie Bale exercising his somewhat dilapidated pantomime horse.
- Los Valentos, Dennis assisted by his wife with their Spanish themed low wire act. The routine included dancing; a one hand horizontal balance, a high kicking walk along the wire, balancing and swaying on a small board laid across the wire, juggling hoops, laying on the wire and passing a small hoop over his body, swaying whilst lying on the Billywire, standing up on one leg from the lying position and finally swaying from side to side whilst balancing on one foot. It was the showmanship and style which made this act a cut above other wire acts with similar tricks.
- Billy Howard's wire walking parody.
- Ballerina on horseback by Joan.
- Charlie Bale as Charlie Chaplin whose efforts to play tiger rag on the trombone all ended in failure. He then played the bagpipes plus a rousing gallop on the post horn. He was then chased from the ring, only to return with his version of a one-man coronation parade. This saw him playing three trumpets together, a side drum and a big bass drum on his back, the drum face being decorated with a crown and the letter ER11 whilst above the drum pole, topped with a crown, carried a Union Jack flag which unfurled as Charlie marched out of the ring.
- Ida with her Pekinese dogs and the mischievous Ki-Ki.

- Rosaire trampoline act with Dennis, Carlos and an unnamed apprentice plus audience participation by some of the children from the audience.

The Rosaire group of lions were not in the show but they were on site, housed in dens alongside the circus. The family at the same time were also providing a circus for an eight-week summer season at none other than Bridlington.

Charlie Bale as Charlie Chaplin

This show was being managed by Joan's parents. When the show opened the lions departed with their presenter Jim Parson his role at Chessington being taken by Dick Carlton.

Though the season ended on the 5 September the Rosaires stayed on for couple of more weeks giving performances whenever there were enough people visiting the zoo.

In addition to the act listed above Joan remembers presenting a trapeze act with her Aunt Ida. However despite the hard work she has very fond memories of her stay at Chessington. 'The evenings were always free as the shows were over by 6 p.m. which meant that there was plenty of time for enjoyment. A lot of young students worked at the zoo. We were a boisterous bunch and had a great time together. There were plenty of cinemas and variety theatres in the vicinity which we would visit regularly.'

In addition to performing at the zoo and in Bridlington they managed to slip in performances at the Royal Hippodrome, Eastbourne and the Aston Hippodrome near Birmingham. What a year!

Eastbourne Gazette 21 January 1953

'The stage of the Royal Hippodrome is barely large enough to create a circus ring, as members of the Rosaires Circus are this week finding out for themselves. On the opening evening the horses, cavorting around the arena, bumped into the perimeter and the Flying Rosaires were quick to find that any high trapeze work would prevent their being seen by the audience.

However, space limitations apart, the circus is a good blend of fun and skill, animal and human antics, which should be enjoyed by old and young alike. A trained llama, circus lions, horses, dogs and even performing geese, vie with tightrope walkers, trapeze artists, dancing girls and the inevitable clowns to provide the laughs and thrills.

Pride of place must go to Capt. Jim Parsons' lions, three savage looking beasts, who nevertheless obey his every word. Equally entertaining are Ida's Pekingese, they pull a cart, ride a scooter and even a tricycle and performing geese, whose military precision might not pass the sergeant-major but it shows what patient training can do.

Thrills on the tightrope are provided by the Los Valentos and on the trapeze by the Flying Rosaire and grace and intelligence by Miss Joan's white horses. The art of the trampoline is made to look much easier than it really is by the Arturos. Acrobatic dancing comes from Marguerite's Acro dolls and humour from Charlie Bale and the clowns.'

1953 – Aston Hippodrome

'I was immensely impressed by Miss Joan Rosaire who represents the third generation of Rosaires, presenting the Liberty Horses and performing on the rings with charm and grace.'

1954 – Ilkeston

'Joan Rosaire daughter of Zena is another talented performer, possessing a charming manner in the ring and she is worthily upholding the family name.'

Eastbourne Gazette 5 January 1955

'Circus Rosaire, which continues for its second and last week at the Royal Hippodrome, completely explodes the myth that a circus cannot be staged on a theatre stage.

There are some amazing examples of animal training from the group of African forest-bred lions and Himalayan bears to the trio of performing geese. Although the lions provide the thrills, for sheer entertainment the geese waddle away with the laughs. Can you imagine the bird you may have had for Christmas dinner see-sawing with another goose or climbing steps and sliding down a Chute and apparently enjoying the fun?

Add a variety of human acts, including the Almada Trio in a clever balancing turn, Los Valentos on the slack wire, 16 years old Carmencita thrilling the audience with her daring trapeze work, the Bouncing Caballeros on the trampoline, Jothia and Joan's smart spinning feats, the Apollos' amazing strong-man act - Apollo alone lifts nine men at once - and you have all that goes to make a real Big Top circus with the advantage of a close-up view from a seat in the theatre.'

1955 – Bridlington

'Applause greeted the entry of Joan Rosaire into the ring of Circus Rosaire with her television horse Goldy, following an announcement that she did so strictly against doctor's orders.

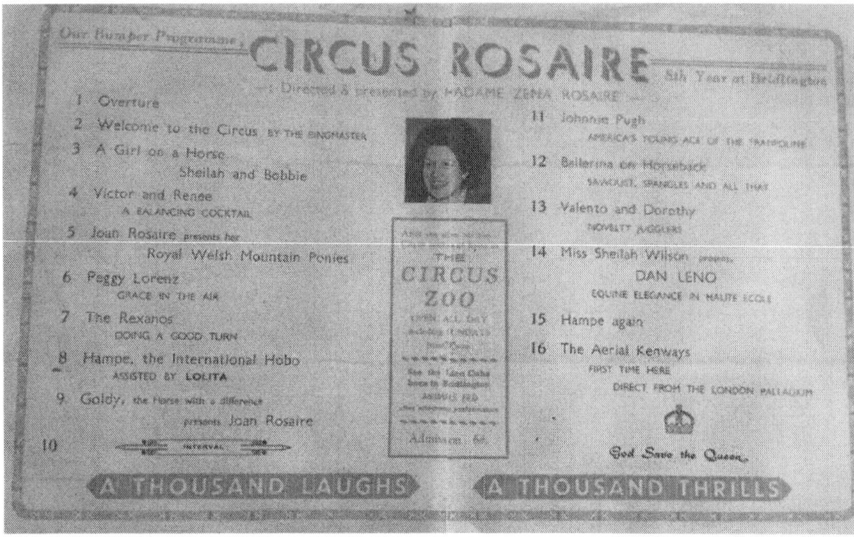
Our Bumper Programme

CIRCUS ROSAIRE

5th Year at Bridlington

Directed & presented by MADAME ZENA ROSAIRE

1 Overture

2 Welcome to the Circus BY THE RINGMASTER

3 A Girl on a Horse
Sheilah and Bobbie

4 Victor and Renee
A BALANCING COCKTAIL

5 Joan Rosaire presents her
Royal Welsh Mountain Ponies

6 Peggy Lorenz
GRACE IN THE AIR

7 The Rexanos
DOING A GOOD TURN

8 Hampe, the International Hobo
ASSISTED BY LOLITA

9 Goldy, the Horse with a difference
presents Joan Rosaire

10 INTERVAL

11 Johnnie Pugh
AMERICA'S YOUNG ACE OF THE TRAMPOLINE

12 Ballerina on Horseback
SAWDUST, SPANGLES AND ALL THAT

13 Valento and Dorothy
NOVELTY JUGGLERS

14 Miss Sheilah Wilson presents
DAN LENO
EQUINE ELEGANCE IN HAUTE ECOLE

15 Hampe again

16 The Aerial Kenways
FIRST TIME HERE
DIRECT FROM THE LONDON PALLADIUM

God Save the Queen

THE CIRCUS ZOO

Admission 6d.

A THOUSAND LAUGHS A THOUSAND THRILLS

Heavily bandaged on her right leg and using a walking stick, she nevertheless put the horse through his paces, though in his enthusiasm he caused her an anxious moment when as part of the routine, he nudged her from behind rather vigorously for her comfort.

Renewed applause showed appreciation of her pluck and skill as eventually Goldy the horse backed carefully from the ring and Joan made her exit.' There were plenty more flattering reviews which showed that Joan had established herself not only as a national but an international circus star by the time she was twenty.

The circus finally closed 1956 soon after their 8th year at Bridlington with Joan in full flow. She presented her Royal Welsh Mountain Ponies, Ballerina Performance and of course Goldy, described as the horse with a difference.

When the circus eventually folded the talented Rosaire family transferred their talents to other circuses and venues around the world and in the years following the Rosaire family leaving the English scene they travelled many hundreds of miles in Europe. From France they toured with d'Hiver, Circo Medrano in Spain, Circo Americano in Porto, Portugal and Circus Price in Madrid. For the summer of 1957 they journeyed with Circo Price from Madrid, down through Portugal and out to the Canary Islands by boat from Lisbon, to stay for some weeks at Las Palmas. With three large cargo boats they sailed out with a very smooth journey but the return was the roughest they ever experienced and at times many thought they would lose their animals.

Still with Circo Price they again visited Lisbon, Porto and Madrid during the winter of 1957/58. Joan had not been as long on the Continent as the rest of the family and it was not until the summer of 1957 that she singled-handed drove a larger Bedford caravan-cum horsebox to the utter amazement of many French and Spanish people on her way to spend the season with Medrano Circus. This followed with Joan with Goldy driving for four days from Madrid to Rapperswil, in Switzerland to join Knie Circus for the 1958 tour from March to November.

I think it is time for Joan to help us with some more of her memories in the circus world and her famous Goldy horses but before I do I would like to finish this chapter with another article by Rupert Croft-Cooke that appeared on a number of the Rosaire programs during the late 1940s: -

'Rosaire's Circus is now acknowledged as the most interesting and picturesque tenting show touting England today and Count Frederick and Countess Rosaire are two of the great personalities of the Sawdust Ring. Truly there never was a family like this one. Four sons and four daughters and every one a performer. You will see Vivienne the exquisite, Ida the intrepid, you will find yourself with laughter at the antics of Jimmy Green, the eldest son of the family and a clown in the great tradition. You will watch Don Valento, the second son whom I regard as one of the three most brilliant wire walkers in the world, and Ivor who can do whatever he likes with Elephants and himself perform wonders on the rings. There is Derrick the youngest, another brilliant performer and the family is supported by some of the finest Circus talent to be found. The whole show is a revelation. I must have seen it myself upwards of a hundred times and I have never known a moment's tedium.

Great characters themselves, the Rosaires have attracted other characters to work with them. Martin Russell Hawkes, a Cambridge man and a Kentish vicar's son, is unique in that he has chosen the profession of lion training from all others because this is the work he is fond of and these are the animals he loves. Charlie Austin one of the great old stagers and Little Freddie a clown in a million.

Wherever Rosaire's Circus goes they leave friends behind them and if you think that in writing in this way about the Rosaires I am gushing, see the show for yourself. I cannot believe that you will not feel its enchantment as I do.'

Chapter 5 - Our Joan with Goldy

Joan with Goldy – 1966

I purchased another of Rupert Croft-Cooke's books on Circus Rosaire 'The Circus has No Home' and in it is a paragraph that describes what Joan was like as a young five year old:- 'At five years old she was the darling and mascot of the whole troupe. Exquisitely formed, her tiny legs in jodhpurs, she would be running in and out of living-wagons or showing off to village children of twice her age, all day. With her thick, long, copper-coloured hair flying behind her, she would balance herself standing on the fat back of a white pony, or order the elephants about, herself unable to reach their knees. I remember how, each of those hot summer afternoons in Yorkshire, she would come into my trailer-caravan and ask for pencil and paper "to draw." And draw she did – her mother on the trapeze, Ivor with the elephants, her grandmother's wagon – chuckling happily at the absurd figures that appeared on the paper. The first of the Rosaire grandchildren, she was already marked for the family profession. It was a question how long Zena would be able to keep her out of the ring. Already on an afternoon when apparatus had been set up for practice and the big tent had been empty for a while, she had been found alone, swinging from the trapeze. No kind of fear in her.'

Just reading this paragraph you cannot come to any other conclusion but that Joan would become a world circus performing star. Joan was literally born on the road on 15 April 1933, in a vehicle driven by her Uncle Aubrey while travelling from Hay-on-Wye to their next venue at Talgarth. Joan is not exactly sure where she was born other than it was in a little Welsh village where they stopped off to find a midwife. Zena though wanted her to be born in England. She is actually registered in Hereford, so the question is. Is she English or Welsh? I'll leave it up to you to decide. There was however concern on the faces in attendance at the appearance of the apparently lifeless body but Florence had no intention of allowing her first grandchild to be born dead. So she slapped and coaxed life into the lifeless body. Celebrations erupted and within the hour Joan was placed upon the back of a pony by her proud grandfather. Her father and mother then led her around in the presence of the circus company. Undoubtedly the earliest contact with a pony accounts for Joan's lifelong love for horses. One of Joan's early nursemaids was Freddie Alice (Little Freddy), a dwarf clown, only 4 foot high. He played a large role in Joan's interest in horses and was with the circus throughout the war. Just for the record Joan's full name is Margaret Joan Leonne Bunning.

Joan was three when she got her first taste of what it was like to perform in front of a large crowd when she appeared in the ring bouncing around on the trampoline as 'Little Miss Yo-Yo.'

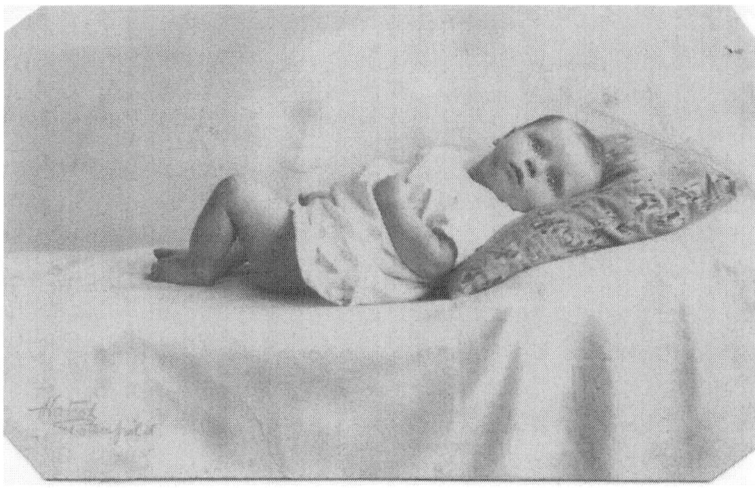

Joan at 9 months

Joan's christening – Saltash, Cornwall – 1933

Children from the audience would be invited to try out tricks on the trampoline, young Joan would go first to show what could be done. She would bounce up and down on the trampoline three times, then drop onto her bottom and bounce back up again. Then the children would have a go. This act of hers did not last long, her Uncle Derrick spotted her with a dirty jumper on and asked her to take it off. She refused, so he banned her from performing, this did not worry Joan as she preferred to play. Shame as she was a healthy red-haired bouncy child but this fit of childish temperament ended her brief career. Joan admits being the first grandchild she was horribly spoilt. 'I would sit in the seats when not performing and tell the audience what was going to happen next.' She would often get kicked out but always found her way back in. On another occasion, still at the tender age of three while some of the family were performing on stage Joan was spotted high up above the stage curtains on one of the fly bars, how she got there nobody knows. Zena her mother fainted when she saw her but somehow Uncle Derrick climbed up and got her under one of his armpits and managed to climb down one handed with the cry 'send her to Zena'. (A fly system, or theatrical rigging system, is a system of rope lines, blocks, bars etc enabling stage crew to move components out of sight of the audience). There is no doubt that she was a little devil and on other occasions she would find her way into the lion's cage, which also caused concerns to the family.

Fly system

Her mother was always working, either performing, practising or carrying out other important circus work, so she would pass Joan around to whoever was available to look after her. One particular lady 'Maria' often got this privilege to look after her while her mother was performing. Maria would often go into the Lions Cage when they were performing and sing. Later Joan was told that this lady was the daughter of the 'Mad' Monk Rasputin. This story seemed a little far-fetched so I decided that a little more research was needed. I was able to find out that one of Rasputin's children 'Maria' had in fact had a short circus career during the 1930s and used to train lions. The story might well indeed be true.

It was another five years before they let Joan back in the ring in a modest High School routine.

Around the age of 4 years her father converted a Daimler bus into a caravan. Joan says: 'It was wonderful compared to the caravans they were used to and her father even had a workshop with a lathe in the back of it, where people would queue up to look in.' Although they still had an outside toilet tent, again as Joan says: - 'In those days it was still not nice to have a toilet in the caravan but my father had to dig a hole at night to empty the toilet into it, it was called "Burying the Parrot" or it was a matter of using the hedges.'

Joan remembers very clearly that from a young age when she had learnt to ride horses, she would help out by riding ponies from place to place and as she explains in the early days the horses and elephants went by road, there was no transport for them. They often pulled the caravans and other vehicles as well. There was as many as 30-40 horses but if she was not on the horses, she was with her uncle Ivor looking after the elephants. Once they reached the next venue the horses would be let loose in a farmer's field that had been acquired for the duration of their stay.

Later when more transport was available, they would have to do double journeys as there were insufficient drivers. Joan particularly remembers driving the monkey cart. There was one particular occasion when Joan was about 15 years of age and was supposedly looking after some of the horses while the others were on route to the next venue but she took the opportunity to have a 'lie in' but the gate had been left open and as Joan puts it 'all our horses said ho ho we are out'.

Still in her bloomers and dressing gown Joan flagged down a passer-by on a motor cycle and asked if had seen any stray horses. He said he had not but was willing to give her a lift along the road. They soon came across the horses on the side verge eating. The problem was that none of the horses had a bridle gear on so Joan took off her dressing gown belt and tied it around the ring leader's nose and safely led them all back to the field. The lead pony just happened to be Tishy who she would later perform on. As you can imagine this was just one of the many incidents that got Joan into trouble.

In the interview with the British Library Joan explained a little more of her grandparents' early life. She understands that their first pony was a pit pony as her grandfather and his two eldest sons worked down the mines in the First World War. Times were hard, money and food scarce but grandmother was an excellent 'scrumpier' and beware if there was a field of turnips nearby.

'Grandad was called Governor by everybody, including Uncle Martin. One day I overheard Uncle Martin say "Governor, what I would really like is to train some lions", "would you my boy, well we shall have to get some for you". Grandad managed to find five young lions for Uncle Martin to look after. He spent many hours in the circus zoo with them, finding names and for them to get accustomed to each other and Uncle Martin.

My father made many props and a cage for the lions to perform in and after many months of careful planning and practice they were ready to perform but not in front of the public. Uncle Martin mustered as many people as possible to sit ringside and make a little noise, slowly increasing the noise as if it was a normal circus audience. Then music was added, with more noise and people moving around. This took several months before the lions were ready to face a real live audience.

At last the day came, everyone on the show was watching from various vantage points around the tent with great excitement. Well perform they did and as far as the audience were concerned with perfection. After the show which was a matinee, all the circus performers were in the back entrance to congratulate the "New Lion Trainer." The atmosphere was like congratulating a new father of twins. The new father was flushed with emotion and happy (Grandad was mighty relieved too). We all had the greatest admiration for Uncle Martin, anybody who has performed before an audience for the first time will realise how special it is but to do it with wild animals is very special indeed.'

Martin and his Lions

Martin's father was Vicar of Sevenoaks and in August 1938 not long after the circus had acquired the lions he came and conducted a service in the ring. The following is a report from the Sheffield Independent: -

'A plain wooden trestle table covered with a cloth and surmounted by two simple candlesticks formed an alter when the Rev. E.A.Hawkes, vicar of Sevenoaks, Kent, conducted a service in the sawdust ring of Rosaire Circus which is now appearing at Whitby. The vicar knelt on a mat placed over the sawdust and sat down on the edge of the circus ring. Eight arc lamps beat down on his head as he conducted the service, while outside the muffled roar of lions and the throbbing of the motor generating the electric current could be heard. In addition to the circus folk, who sat on chairs round the ring, the circus seats were filled with hundreds of visitors and residents.

The vicar's son Mr. Martin Hawkes, who is the circus lion tamer, sat with his colleagues in the ring. His mother accompanied the hymns on a harmonium. The service was held by the Reverend in gratitude of the circus people for befriending his son and he had travelled specially from Sevenoaks with Mrs Hawkes to see Martin doing his act with five lions.'

In February 1939 just a few months prior to Martin marrying Ida he was attacked in a London theatre by a lion which tore his left hand but was able to carry on to the end of the act. It was around about this time that Joan spent many an hour listening to Uncle Martin telling her about how animals behaved and how he trained them. Martin was a trained vet.

'When the Second World War started, Uncle Martin's father expected him to enlist. This he did attaining the rank of Major. It was also a very sad time for the circus, the town where we had our winter quarters insisted that the lions were destroyed in case they escaped during an air raid. Obviously, nobody attached to the circus wanted this to happen but public opinion overruled and we had them shot. It was a very traumatic time for everybody connected with the show.'

The town was Billericay in Essex, the area was on the flight path of the German aeroplanes returning from their missions of bombing London, so it was quite feasible for this to happen and in fact a bomb did drop in the field behind the farm. The flight path was known as Bomb Alley.

As you would expect it was very difficult for circus performers when they were young to get a normal education. The circus elders did their best but as you can imagine Joan's education was very fragmented. Her first school was Green Street Green primary school, Orpington, Kent. Joan like many children cried on her first day when left by her mother. However, being rather strong-willed she walked home at playtime only to be taken back but then walked home again in the afternoon. The following day she was back at school.

Joan was about 4 years old at the time so after a couple of days it was decided to wait until she was a little older. Joan was about 6 years old before she went back and had another attempt of going to school this time it was during the winter period back in Billericay.

The school was the local junior school 'Quilters' and the one teacher there Joan remembers was Miss Gentry. Although only 6 years old she was allowed to go to school by herself as the caravans were parked on the field at the back of Archer Hall and there were only fields to cross. She remembers on one occasion when walking home on her own the air raid siren sounded, she put on her gas mask and threw herself into a nearby ditch. She didn't want the Germans to get her! Rather a scary moment for a 6-year-old. On another occasion a couple of young boys threw a brick and it hit Joan on the back of head, it did hurt.

Zena at the time was working with elephants at Belle Vue, Manchester so it was back to her Aunt Ida, who was living in Tye Common Road, Billericay in a bungalow named 'Tylands'. More on her education later. Joan never went to a senior school.

'When I was six years old my mother and father worked for a season on Madam Clara Paulo's circus. She was a formidable lady and I, like many others, was totally in awe of her. She ran the circus single-handed and with a rod of iron! She didn't seem at all like my own Grandma Rosaire who rather doted on me! I realise now of course that there were certain similarities. They both had large families, an extremely hard way of life and had to be very much in command of the situation.

Her daughter Emily Thomson was in charge of the liberty ponies and that summer was breaking in a new troupe. All the Paulo children were enlisted to ride the ponies at practice and I was also allowed to ride. A lot of giggling went on as we juggled up and down on the bare backs of the little horrors. I seemed to spend more time clinging on or falling off. I don't think I was a lot of help but it was a lot of fun! The Paulos had some beautiful animals, lots of coloured ring horses. They were famous for them and their riding acts.'

Zena, Ida, Emily Paulo, John Swallow – Salt and Sauce

Joan about this time became ill with tonsillitis and had to have an operation. Joan explains: - 'On the occasion when the circus was in Luton in a very nice park near a boating lake, I was suffering with a painful throat, which turned out to be tonsillitis. The doctor said that I needed an operation to get rid of my tonsils but there was no room at the local hospital. He asked if there was a large enough table in any of the caravans for him to operate on. My mother invited him to come and see, this he did and the only table large enough was the one in the lions' cage. So, he arranged for his team to come down early next morning to scrub it down and get things ready for the operation. When it was ready my mother took me in my pyjamas into the circus tent, I climbed on to the table, laid down and something like a tea cosy was put over my face and something that smelt awful was put on it. I didn't remember anything else until I woke after the operation with a dreadful sore throat.

The next day I sneaked off and went boating, I was having a splendid time but my mother was getting very worried because she did not know where I was. She sent everybody out looking for me but, in the meantime, although happy I was very tired so I laid down in the bottom of the boat and fell asleep. The local park keeper found me and returned me to my mother who then banned me from leaving our caravan for the rest of our stay in that park. I was not very happy about this but at least my mother knew where I was.'

Joan as we know was the only grandchild for the first five or six years and one would assume that playtimes were a little lonely for her but no, as Joan explains: - 'I had my animals to entertain me, horses, boxing kangaroo, racoons, elephants and Queenie my pet dog who I used to dress up, she must have thought I was a pest. There was also the elephant's barrel of water where I would go and a have swim, quite often fully clothed, that used to get me into trouble. I used to make friends with the local children very easily. They would come flocking into the circus grounds wherever we pitched up and helped out doing odd jobs, we referred to them as Chinese labour. When my cousins came along, I taught them all to ride, so no I was not lonely.'

Joan's grandparents Bunnings, had a dairy farm (Manor Farm) in Walsoken, Norfolk. When Joan was about eight her grandfather Bunning died. So, for a short time the family left the show and went up to look after grandmother Bunning and the farm. While there Ted made the farm milkman a milking stall, he used to take it everywhere with him and tell people that his boss made it for him. Joan's parents thought it was an opportunity to send Joan to the local school. After a short stay Zena and Ted returned to the show leaving Joan behind to further her education but as Joan says this was not very successful and she also soon returned.

Joan at 4/5 years old on Tishy

By the time Joan was five the Count had given her 'Tishy' a Welsh-Shetland pony and it was not long before she was training the pony in a High School Act. Tishy was approximately 11 hands, typical of the Shetland breed, with a fairly large but nice head and rather short legs, a rotund stomach the result of several foals. To Joan she was a Pegasus, to everyone else she was a bit of a pest! She could untie knots and get out of anywhere. She was the daughter of one of Derrick Rosaire's two black Shetlands that he performed a riding act with when he was a small boy. Joan loved the pony to distraction.

'My grandfather used to tack her up for me and take me with him wherever he went, which sometimes meant a visit to the local pub where I would wait outside with a packet of crisps and a glass of lemonade! Sheer bliss! As I grew older and was more capable of handling Tishy on my own, I began to have ambitions of becoming a world-famous high school rider.

Joan and Tishy – Chester 1945

I started to train her in secret but everybody knew. I learned how to get Tishy to perform a trick by using reflexes and giving a great deal of praise and reward, not by punishment by hitting but by withholding the reward. I soon realised that horses and animals for that matter are more intelligent at picking up body language than humans and if you were not feeling too good yourself this would be passed on to the animal. They appeared to love performing in front of a big and responsive audience, enjoying the applause. Horses would often prick their ears back as a sign of appreciation.

I think my ambition was fired by the fact that John Swallow who had the famous elephant duo, Salt and Sauce also had a rather splendid cream horse named Tony, with which he did an excellent high school routine. Tony had a wonderful nature – so good indeed that I was allowed to ride him around outside the tent after his act, to cool him down.' 'Uncle' Johnnie Swallow as Joan often referred to him was an archetypal showman of his day and brought a little polish and style to Circus Rosaire. John was in fact Joan's godfather.

Poor old Tishy though, she had to suffer me quite a bit in those early days but she got her own back in many ways! She also taught me a lot about horses and their idiosyncrasies. It was when I was seven or eight that my career really started to take off riding Tishy in a high school act I had trained her to do, this culminating in jumping over a fire pole out of the ring. The very first performance somebody had been a little over-zealous with the fire and Tishy gave the most enormous leap, completely jumping me off. I landed on my derriere but very quickly remounted successfully. I don't suppose it was much of an act but as I was only young and riding an immaculate small white pony, the novelty of it went down well.'

It was also around this time that Joan found a mongrel ginger dog wondering around Billericay. To Joan's disappointment somebody claimed it but grandfather (the Count) stepped in and bought it from the person for £1.00. Joan immediately set about training it to ride Tishy and not surprisingly, she named the dog Ginger.

Over the next few years Joan became more involved in the circus routine, taking responsibility for her Aunt Ida's Pekinese, taking control of the panatrope and controlling the show's music with meticulous care. Her Uncle Ivor allowed her on occasions to make guest appearances with his famous elephants, Salt and Sauce. She also made appearances with the

Liberty ponies (though they had a harness on they did not have anybody on their backs as they marched around the ring), and she also had a few breath-taking moments in the cage of lions with Uncle Martin.

As hinted Joan was a bit of a devil and she was often threatened with boarding school, this used to bring her down to earth in two seconds flat but when she was about 8 years old she was sent to live with a friend of the family, Annie Brailsford in Bottisford, Nottinghamshire in another attempt to give her some schooling, this lasted for six months.

The circus then spent two winters in a scrap yard at Twyford, Berkshire, the owners were more than happy to have them there and even had stables built. This meant for two winters Joan found herself cycling every day to Twyford Wargrave Memorial School. Joan hated it and admits that she was no scholar and regrets that she did not try harder, now realising it helps an enormous lot if you get a formative schooling in your early years.

As the family grew through marriage there were too many for a small circus so several of the sons and daughters went and found fame elsewhere but often returned when needed.

'During the Second World War my grandfather "The Count" was still walking the horses from town to town and some of the happiest times were riding the journeys with him. He would be driving a big red and white stallion called Carlos, who was quite a handful, so much so that often granddad would himself walk leading the horse for most of the journey until it settled down. Carlos was powerful and now on reflection potentially very dangerous. I think he was sold eventually to some gypsies.'

As already mentioned, fuel for vehicles was rationed so journeys became shorter also food was on rations, sugar scarce. The various acts had to often manage their own props as many of the men on the show and backroom staff had been called up to serve in the forces, something unheard of under normal circumstances. It was left to the wives and women to get the show around. They all did the build-up and pull downs and drove the Lorries that contained the show's equipment.

There were also many unusual events taking place at this time for example the bright lights on the circus tent could not be used as it made a target for enemy aeroplanes, it was strange to see the usually brightly lit up show front in almost complete darkness, though customers accepted it in good spirit, they were just delighted to think that we would not let the enemy get us down.

On occasions, the men would come home on leave, bringing friends with them and this would make life easier for the girls. They would also perform in the show, making the performance full of sparkle with their sheer 'joie de vivre' (joy of living) at being once more in their right place – in the ring.

The Baker boys and the Kayes and others would also spend their leaves with them – performing in riding acts, all competing against each other. The horses they rode were: - old Susie a red and white with a Roman nose but she ran like clockwork and Sally, who belonged to Tommy Bale. Years later Joan rode both Susie and Sally in a riding act.

There was also Duke. He was a very fast pony. Derrick used him as a finishing horse and he did jumps over bars. Duke was also my Ida's voltige horse. Ida was the fastest voltige rider Joan ever saw. Joan later did voltige on Duke and taught her two younger cousins David and Carlos Rosaire to vault on him.

During these war years they took money in whatever way possible. Joan set up a Pet's Corner which included, Rabbits, Goats, Pigs, with the main attraction being a giant rat, actually a Coypus, charging 6d entrance fee. On one occasion a gentleman came by and said would she like a water otter, the answer being yes, he said he would return. Several weeks went by, no water otter then a large parcel turned up for Joan. She thought that this was a little strange a water otter wrapped up but no it was an 'Old Kettle'. As Joan says: 'some people are strange.'

Joan goes on to say: - 'Zena my mother was a very wonderful artist, she performed on the rings, similar to the trapeze but very much more difficult. She would not let me do the rings as it was extremely hard for a woman but allowed me to do the trapeze.

My Aunt Ida performed on the trapeze, she worked in an extraordinary way – very fast – which suited her temperament. To give Aunt Ida a breather, I used to do a few tumbling tricks on the ground below the trapeze to give her time to catch her breath. Then perform a couple of tricks whilst Aunt Ida held me, that is, until I learned to do the tricks on the trapeze myself. I then opened the act with my normal pace routine and Aunt Ida took over her part to finish.'

The Trapeze Artists

A trio of acrobats enter the ring
Their sequined leotards shimmering,
They climb the ladders to reach up high
Unhook the swings and begin to fly.

Fearlessly hanging with arms at the ready,
Legs tightly hooked keeping nice and steady.
An acrobat launches in mid air
To be caught by hands reaching there.

The crowd gasps with wonder to watch them twist
And spin through the air with a flick of a wrist.
We crane our necks to watch the show,
Then they tumble and dive to the net below.

By Sue Ranford
(Basildon Borough heritage Society)

'By the time the war ended I was twelve years old, I was now riding Voltige and in the trapeze act, actually performing on the trapeze, not just doing things on the ground to give Aunt Ida a breather but it was always my ambition to work more with horses and it was not long before I was allowed to present the two white liberty horses, "Betsy and Billy". Now I felt I was getting somewhere.'

'Betsy belonged to grandad and I probably owe my whole career to her. She was a beautiful little Arab mare, the leader of the liberty troupe. She also went in harness and her speciality spot was "The Educated Horse." She was billed as "Betsy the Horse with the Human Brain." All the family had presented her and by the time it came to my turn, Betsy knew every trick in the trade! She was extremely intelligent. If she didn't feel like working, she would go inexplicably lame. She would also scarper out of the back entrance before the act and nothing or no one could catch her until the show was over. Then she would give herself up! But she was a wonderful schoolmistress; she taught me to ad lib, bless her. No other horse caused me more frustration but also gave me that wonderful sense of achievement when it all went right.'

Joan with Betsy and Billy

'By 1945 my parents were now getting even more worried about my lack of education, when one of our many friends, who happened to be a very fine horse man, in fact quite a famous horse man came to visit. While talking to Zena and Dad, it was suggested that I go and stay with them for a tenting season and go to school. It was also about this time that I was kicking my heels to some extent, I was neither a child nor an adult. So, after some deliberation it was decided that I should go, so that I could go to school as well as being taught to ride horses correctly with a saddle and compete in jumping competitions. I was delighted with the arrangement. The friend and his wife had a small daughter so off I went to stay with them in a small village in Cheshire.

It was all very strange to start with but I soon settled in, looking after the animals and finding my way around the farm. 'Uncle' Curly as he was known had very good competent staff which comprised of a Cowman, Farmhand and a Horse groom, called 'Doug' who I remember as being kind and sympathetic when I felt home sick.'

'Uncle' Curly, in fact was Mr Alfred Beard. He taught Joan the art of show jumping and much about the rearing and training of racehorses. Curly was a member of the first British show jumping team to go abroad after the war. However, Joan did not manage to go to school, but of course whenever the Rosaire's Circus was in the locality she visited the show.

'Whilst I was there, I was introduced to yet another aspect of horsemanship and will be forever grateful to the Beards for giving me that opportunity. I rode some very famous horses of their day. There was a beautiful chestnut called Bartestree. He was named after the village he came from in Hertfordshire, not far from where I was born, so I always felt an affinity with him. He was a fantastic jumper – to ride him over a jump was like flying!

There were so many horses at the Beards that it's hard to remember them all but there is one I shall never forget. Her name was Vixen, a 14.2 hand chestnut mare. I made my debut in a show jumping ring on her. She was a marvellous jumper but very hot natured and very hard to stop!

Uncle Curly on Monty

I was fortunate to win a few junior show jumping events but my first was a nightmare. Waiting to enter the arena for the first time for my round was worse than any "first night" nerves I had ever experienced! As I stood there with the groom holding the pony's head to steady her, my stomach in my mouth, I wondered what I was doing so far from the circus. Suddenly we were off, the first fence over, approaching the next, then another. By now we had gained a bit of speed. I took a strong pull – nothing happened! We flew the next fence and now the brakes had failed completely. I finished the course but kept going. The second time round the groom stepped into the ring and made a flying tackle, like a hero in a western and I was finally pulled to a halt. The pony jumped clear but we were eliminated. Oh, the shame of it! I still blush to this day but as I gained experience, I won some very good competitions on her.'

Prior to Joan joining 'Uncle' Curley, Uncles Derrick and Ivor had taught Joan to vault and trick ride, so by the time she went to 'Uncle' Curley's farm she could vault onto big horses and Curley would hold bets with his friends how big a horse Joan could get on and as Joan says: - 'I earned him a bit of money.'

'When I finally returned home to the circus, our ponies seemed very tame by comparison. So I used to liven up our Sundays (non-working days) by organising jumping competitions in the ring with the liberty ponies. By Monday, those of us who had taken part would be stiff and sore from this unusual pastime, until grandad quite rightly put a stop to it!'

Joan had spent approximately two years with 'Uncle' Curley and it was soon afterwards when Joan was about 15 years of age when she was travelling along a road in Wales near Llanberis, at the foot of Mount Snowdon with her mother from their last venue on their way to Hereford when her life was to take another turn.

'It was very early in the morning but the sun was already rising, it looked like being a nice day. My mother suddenly shouted, "Joan look over there," I said "if I do, we could well end up in a ditch." I was driving, my mother was teaching me to drive, as we were travelling very early in the morning there was very little chance of there being any traffic, also mother had hurt her shoulder and it was very painful for her to steer the car another reason for me doing so. We pulled onto the grass verge and stopped, mother said "look in that field, there's a beautiful creamy coloured horse." I believe it's called a Palomino. Sure enough, there in a field stood a lovely horse, its coat gleaming in the early sunshine. "So, what now" I asked, "Well when we get to the next place, why not come back with Uncle Martin (who was a registered practicing vet) and see if you can buy it." So that is exactly what we did. Uncle Martin asked the farmer who owned it would he be willing to sell it, he said yes and we bought it for

£60.00, all my savings. The horse was an unbroken four-year-old and did not have a name but in my mind, I had already got a name for it but I needed to discuss it first with my mother.

Painting of Goldy

The transaction finished, Uncle Martin and I returned to the circus which was in Abergavenny, not far from where I was born in the town of Hereford. I managed to persuade her to enter the horse box back to the show. On the following journey, however she would have none of it and refused to get into it, so I had no choice but to walk her 12 miles along the road to the next town. Within a week I was able to box the lively filly, after which

I had no more trouble with her. She turned out to be a remarkably quick learner, she was performing in public within twelve weeks.

To me it seemed fate was now playing a part. I named her Goldy (many journalists and others often spelt the name Goldie but I have kept to Joan's spelling) and now I had to get her used to Circus life. After everybody had been to visit and admire her, I decided that I would teach her to be rope and stake trained, something all horses were. It allowed them to grass graze and not be in a horse tent all day. It did not take long for Goldy to be roped and staked as she was a very intelligent horse. I always had her in my sight or Mother would deputise for me (Mother was a very accomplished horsewomen) and it did not take long for Goldy to adapt to our way of living.'

For a couple of years after the war with the boys returning to the circus, they rebranded themselves as the 'Rosaire Brothers Circus' and as we see Joan gets herself on the programme with Betsy.

One of Joan's most terrifying moments was in 1948 when the circus was in Jersey. They were set up on the sea front at St Helen, the big top was up, the seats had been wired together to stop people knocking them over, an early health and safety requirement. The on the Saturday a very strong gale blew up, blowing down the big top and other tents. It was made worse by the fact that the seats were wired together, therefore not allowing the staff to lower them, resulting in the tents getting badly torn.

Joan remembers leading all the ponies away to the end of the ground and tying them up to railings. However, working with the circus at the time was a French horse performer 'Count Delarmore' who had a dozen thoroughbred liberty horses. Their tent had fallen on them and the Count was panicking, so Joan with the Count's groom unravelled them from the tent and led them down to the end of the ground and tied them up to the railings next to the circus ponies who were taking it all in their stride. Joan had jumped on one of the horses to find it was the only one that had not been broken in but as Joan says: - 'It was broken in by the time we got to the end of the ground and safety.'

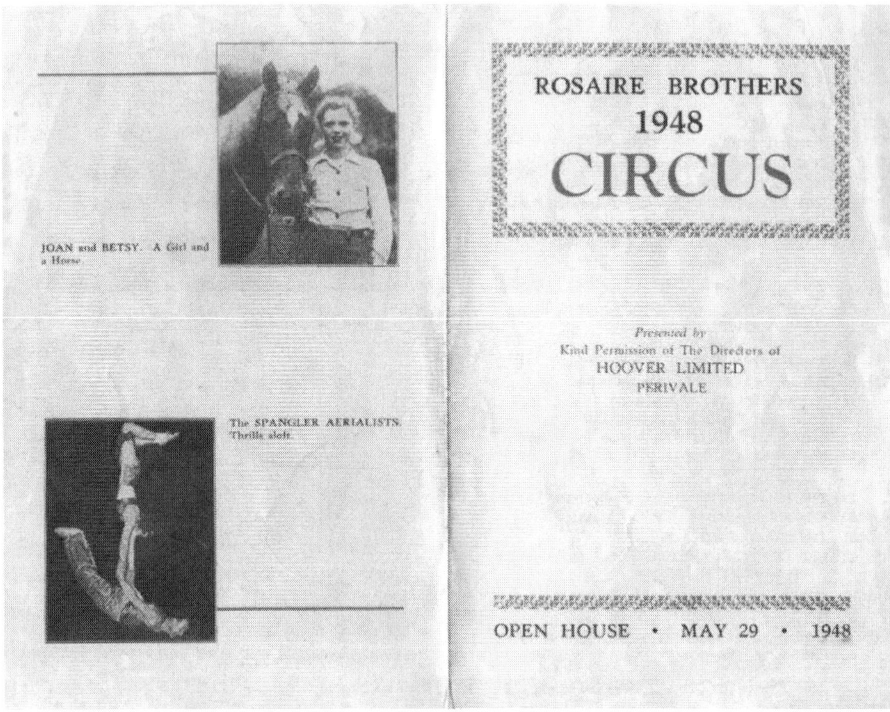
JOAN and BETSY. A Girl and a Horse

The SPANGLER AERIALISTS. Thrills aloft.

ROSAIRE BROTHERS
1948
CIRCUS

Presented by
Kind Permission of The Directors of
HOOVER LIMITED
PERIVALE

OPEN HOUSE • MAY 29 • 1948

Joan and Betsy – A girl and a Horse

On Sunday they called in a sailmaker and he spent all day repairing the tents with the help of Zena to make sure they were ready for the Monday performance.

Around this time Derrick's wife's brother, Tommy Kayes was a very well-known Lion Trainer, who had a very extraordinary opening to his act. He would first bow to the audience then go to enter the lions cage, the lions would all rush to the opening and appear to go crazy, jumping up and down and would not let Tommy into the cage. It was very wild and frightening and it was known for some women in the audience to faint.

Blow down in Jersey 1948

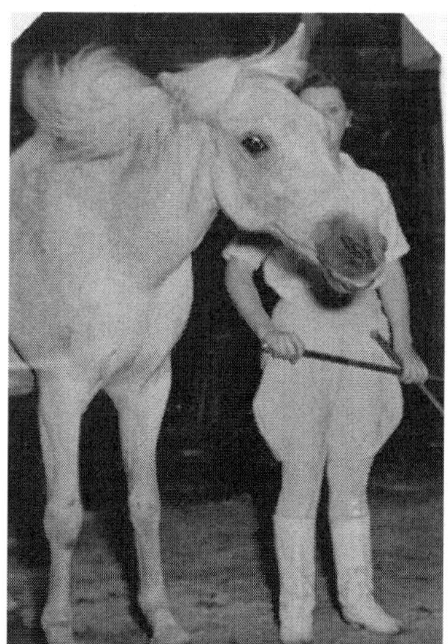

Betsy with Joan Jersey 1948

Joan and Duke – Jersey 1948

Zena, Charlie Bexkett, Dennis and Emelia Jersey 1948

‘Also following Uncle Derrick’s marriage to Betty he no longer performed on a regular basis on Grandfathers Circus, he used to go with other shows if he got a better offer with his three acts. One with a dog act he copied from his sister Ida which consisted of a Pekinese which was quite a rarity in those days. He also had a wonderful performing bear called Mini and a golden Palomino Horse, “Tony” who he did an extraordinary act with.

However, when he was out of work, he would return to Grandfather’s Circus, the problem was that when he left Grandfather’s show it would leave a hole in the programme. Uncle Derrick had been the main presenter of animals but he never taught me how to train animals but that never stopped me watching him in practice. Every opportunity I got, I would watch the practise and ask questions. I must have been a right little pest. He never really found time to stop and talk to a precocious child. I nevertheless picked up quite a lot of valuable knowledge. I was always practicing on my poor dog, Queenie. She must have wondered what was going to happen next. She put up with it all so very good natured.

I loved the act he did with his horse Tony and I decided I would do a similar act. I started to train Goldy to do this. As stated she was a quick learner but I could feel there was something not quite right about this for me, I soon realised what it was, Tony was performing with a man and a very talented one at that but when I presented Goldy, I was doing it as Uncle Derrick did, this was not very ladylike, so I tried a different tactic which I felt was more fitting for me and Goldy. I did however teach Goldy all Tony’s routines.

He had a wonderful line in his patter, he would call Tony “Funny Face” and Tony would chase him out of the ring. I altered this for Goldy who would push me out of the ring and then come back on her own and take a bow. By now I felt Goldy and I were ready to make our debut but when the day came I was very excited and a little frightened.

My mother gave me excellent advice as she always did. Just treat it like a practice, you must not convey your fright to Goldy, she will be great, she is a very intelligent animal, now get in the ring and make me proud.

The ring door curtains opened and we were on our way. I have to say, I cannot remember all the details now but I guess it must have been okay. We received a good applause and Goldy taking her bow on her own went down exceedingly well.' Goldy became known as the Wonder Horse and their routine was as follows: -

They would enter into centre of the ring, Goldy nods and Joan would say 'Ladies and Gentlemen, boys and girls this is my friend Goldy. Goldy say hello to everyone' horse nods 'Now I want you to show them how you do a nice waltz' horse pirouettes, into centre & nods.

'Show everyone how you stand like Rocking Horse, now rock a little that was a little!! Rock a little more!! OK now let's have a nice march.'

'When I take this off (bridle) you won't go away will you?' 'Show everyone how you say YES....by nodding your head, Ok...now how do you say NO....Good now show them how you move your lips & speak...whisper in my ear...Oh you feel tired!! Would you like to lie down then?'

Horse nods yes. Lies down, sits up, gets up and behaves like a wild stallion!! Rears into centre. Crosses legs.

'Have you finished your performance? Horse nods yes, then I have a little present for you but what do I get for it? Kisses.' 'Ok once around the ring and out you go' refuses to go,

'Come here to me, would you like to show everyone how you leave the ring backwards? Horse does nothing, repeat last sentence, horse still does nothing ...Have you suddenly gone deaf? Horse nods yes!'

'I walk to front of ring with Goldy, he kisses me a couple of times, then backs halfway, I call him Funny Face, he chases me, then backs all the way, nods I walk forward to take a call,

Goldy comes up behind me and pushes me out of the ring. We both return and take final call. Exit.'

'Zena was right as usual, I must say without her help and advice, I would definitely not have achieved any of my subsequent success. I must explain why I called my mother by her Christian name, it was because as a young child, I would be left alone on occasions, for instance when she was performing in the ring and I would be left with one or other of the family who claimed that I was an absolute PEST. As my mother's act ended in the ring, who ever had charge of me, would say, for goodness sake "take it to Zena." My mother, however was quite happy for me to call her Zena and I did so for the rest of her life.

Goldy speaking to Joan

To me she was a most remarkable women, she reared all the baby animals we had including our lion cubs. Many people told her she would not be able to rear them unless she had the "Colostrum" which is the first milk from the mother lioness.

Well she proved them wrong! Our Lioness 'Ranee' would have the cubs but if they were not taken away from her pretty rapidly, she would have killed them. One of the ladies with the show at the time was pregnant and had been provided with National Dried Milk, which was not of exceptional quality but turned out to be suitable for the lion cub's digestion. Zena managed to rear five cubs on it very successfully. It was apparent that all the baby animals looked upon her as their mother.'

Goldy pushing Joan around

It did not however take long for various manufacturers of baby milk to try and cash in. The following is an advert that appeared on one of Circus Rosaire's programmes for Ostermilk produced by Glaxo Laboratories Ltd. Which no doubt helped to pay for the printing of the programme.

'Ranee' who was a six-year-old African Lioness was one of the stars of the show she would be led on to the stage by Zena who allowed the children to gracefully pat her. However, Ranee's thunder on one occasion was quickly stolen by her small cub which had only been born a week before but as stated she disliked her cubs so much that she pushed her away. Joan and Zena stepped in and took over the mother's job with the aid of a baby's bottle. Joan for a few nights took it to bed with her. 'She tore my pyjamas to sheds, but she's the nicest Christmas present I could have had,' said Joan.

In fact, Joan appeared on the BBC radio programme 'In Town Tonight' after the BBC obviously got to hear of the Lion Cub.

The announcer, John Ellison introduced Joan as follows: -

John – 'Even in the entertainment world these days there are not many family businesses left but the Rosaire Circus which opens at the Chelsea Palace on Monday is one of them. So, when there's an addition to the family in the shape of a lion cub, it's a really happy event. Here is Joan Rosaire to tell us about how she's bringing it up.'

Zena and the cub

John – Why are you bringing it up, Miss Rosaire?

Joan – His mother is a very fine lioness but a very bad mother and half an hour after he was born she tossed him out of her den. I happened to catch him as he fell. I wrapped him in my cardigan to keep him warm and took him to my caravan.

John –Did you have any difficulty in feeding him?

Joan – Yes, he was very weak, he couldn't take a bottle, so I filled my mouth with milk and sort of fed him off my tongue. When he got stronger, he took to the bottle.

John – Where does he sleep?

Joan – At the moment with me in the caravan. He's a month old now and I hope to have him for another three months.

John – What do you do in the circus?

Joan – In a small family business you have to be prepared to do anything but I love training horses and riding bareback. I've been in the lion's cage two or three times but I don't like it and I've worked the trampoline and the trapeze. Once the trapeze gave way in a theatre and I nosedived into the orchestra pit.

John – Did you hurt yourself?

Joan – No I fell on something soft. I think it was the trumpeter. It amused the audience.

John – What are you going to call your lion cub?

Joan – Well, I've brought him with me tonight and as this is his first London appearance, I thought I'd name him after 'In Town Tonight'.

John – You can't call him that – it's too long!

Joan – Yes you are right we intend calling it Simba

John – A good choice, Joan Rosaire, thank you for coming along tonight, I hope you get home okay and he does not stop London's traffic.

Joan with new born cub, Simba

'The children around the circus also loved to be around my mother, she would tell them stories, keeping them amused for hours. Wherever she went with the lion cubs, children followed her. They also loved her rock buns and apple pies, she was a very good cook. Above all she was a very accomplished performer. In all my time in the circus, I never came across another person who was able to perform as many acts as she could. This included, Rings, Trapeze, Bareback riding, High School riding, Trampoline and also presenting performing animals of all breeds including elephants.

However, as you would gather it was her lions and cubs in particular, she was very fond off. One lion cub lived with them until it was two years old. Unfortunately, it got so big and strong and if you mistakenly stood say on its tail, it would turn and grab your ankle, a painful experience. Eventually all the lion cubs were sold to Robert Bros circus, it was a very upsetting time for Zena.'

Zena with one of the cubs and children

Just prior to Joan's 16th birthday, Zena told her to get a bridle and go down to Billericay Station where there was something waiting for her. Waiting for her was the pony 'Vichy'. It had travelled from Twyford, Berkshire. Joan was thrilled and it was 'Vichy' that she practised and performed her Ballerina acts on.

Zena with a growing lion cub in the Local

By now Joan at the tender age of sixteen had become an accomplished circus artist, whether it was parading with the Liberty Horses, up on the trapeze with her aunts or helping Aunt Ida with her Pekinese Dogs, performing with Betsy, but with this first performance with Goldy under her belt she knew that her time had come to become a circus star in her own right. Although she maintained that it was her horses and in particular Goldy who were the real stars.

Though only 16, Joan decided to go on strike for more money. Finances were always tight, money came in only through the box office from which expenses had to be paid, then the artists and any money left over was shared between the proprietors. Joan at the time was not a proprietor nor an engaged artist and was only paid 10 shillings a week. Joan was struggling to make ends meet as she spent most of the money on her horses. She was also doing two to three acts per show, so she asked for £2.00 per week. She was ignored so she went on strike she soon got the £2.00 per week

Who's The Boss - From Joan's collection of drawings.

Later when many were getting £10.00 per show, plus food and accommodation, Joan with her two to three acts per show was doing much more than the rest of them so her wages were eventually raised to £6.00 per week. In 1949 Ivor left the show and in 1953 Dennis left the show for Australia with little warning so Joan now found herself not only doing three acts per show, she was acting as groom, driver, working the box office and involved in anything that needed doing. Although still poorly paid for the work she was doing, her wages were increased to £10.00 per week so she was at least earning some money for herself.

Sometime during the late 1940s Joan met up with a young girl, Gaye Jones. Gaye was around 17 years old at the time and was performing with an all-female acrobatic troupe known as Acromaids (4 girls). They had had a winter season performing with the Rosaires in various theatres around the country. Dennis Rosaire was obviously impressed with Gaye and asked her to come down to Billericay and try out trampoline. This she did and Dennis took her on whereby she would join him and his son Carlos whenever they performed on the trampoline.

It was at Billericay she first met Joan and they soon became firm friends, a friendship that has lasted all their lives, even sharing the same birthdate. It was not long before Joan asked Gaye whether she could ride. Gaye's response was 'no' then out of the side of her mouth said 'Well we will soon remedy that' at which Gaye was thrown over a horse and led around Billericay by Joan until she could manage the horse herself. In those early days there were very few cars, so they could gallop around anywhere they liked. The horse was 'Duke' and was to be Gaye's companion for the rest of her time with the Rosaire family which lasted for approximately seven to eight years. Gaye lived with the family in a large caravan built by Joan's father at the farm in Billericay.

Gaye goes on to explain: -'Now I was working with Joan, we spent most of our time with the horses, up in the mornings cleaning out the stables and grooming them, before stopping for lunch. Sometimes we found a few hours in the afternoon to go to the local cinema or shopping before going back for the shows in the evening. This routine happened whether we were at home in Billericay or at the various venues around the country. In February 1952 we were ready to go to the cinema in Doncaster but on this occasion, we heard that King George V1 had died and as one would expect the cinema and shops were closed.

Joan on another occasion noticed I had not had my ears pierced, she soon remedied that by piercing my ears with a darning needle.'

Gaye also explained that during the winter seasons when playing in theatres they would find stables for the animals and because there was very little traffic and lighting on the roads until long after the war, they would ride home at night. 'Joan would lead riding Goldy and leading one liberty horse either side. I would follow behind with Duke and leading Billy the Llama on one side and a small pony on the other side.

Gaye on Duke

On one occasion when walking home in Walthamstow a door opened on the other side of the road and a light shone out. This resulted in Billy breaking free and racing across the road into a nearby cafe causing untold havoc. Screams and breaking crockery could be heard, it took us some time to organise the horses so Joan could go and rescue Billy and apologise to the landlord. The following day the landlord notified the local paper and gained some publicity for himself and us.'

Joan remembers that Billy, like other llamas were one of the few animals that were difficult to train and in the main they used to just allow them to walk into the ring, often during the interval period to amuse the children, although she did train one of her dogs to ride on Billy's back. Where or how Billy was acquired Joan does not know. Her grandfather just came home from a pub one night with it.

Billy the Llama with Dennis

Bridlington was one of the circus's favourite places they visited. The following are a few of the letters that have appeared in the Bridlington Free Press.

Ken Ward - (25 February 2008).

'I used to work at Postill's Riding School in Fortyfoot and when the circus came each summer in a field next door I used to spend all my spare time at night and weekends at the circus. I helped out with the horses, Vichy and Goldy, as well as helping with all aspects of circus life, such as helping in the ring with the clowns and with a father and two sons who did a strongman act.

The year the lion cub Rajah was born I used to help bottle feed him, groom him and take him for walks on a chain. He was my constant companion for the 16 weeks the circus was there and he became a real pet. On one occasion he was taken to Garnett's Poodle parlour in Lansdowne Road to have a dry shampoo as a publicity stunt. He started sucking Mr Garnett's finger and would not let go, so I was called from work to sort out the situation, to Mr Garnett's relief, as nobody else could handle him like me. He was a very beautiful placid lion and when he eventually went to Bristol Zoo, they said they had never known a lion that was so friendly with humans. At the time he left Bridlington he could stand on his back legs, put his front paws on my shoulders and lick my face, I was 6ft 3in at that time. Joan's mother Zena was always very kind to me and I had many meals and happy times with the family in their caravan.

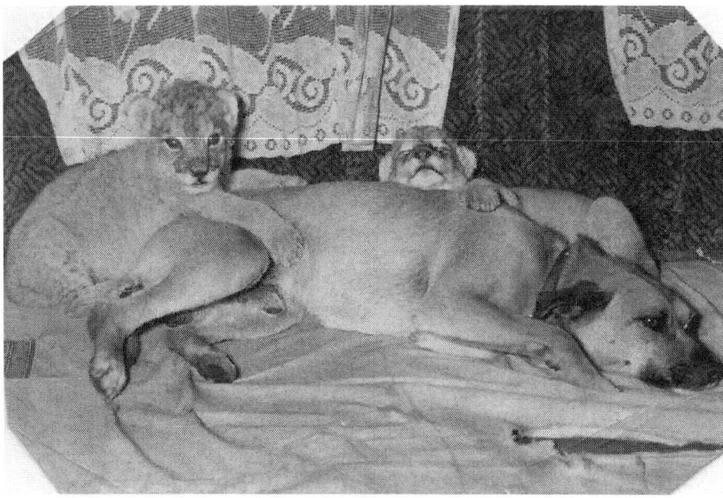

Cubs and dog at Bridlington – 1956

It was a sad loss to me and Bridlington when the circus no longer came for the summer season but it left me with lifelong memories of wonderful times. I hope you can send my best wishes and regards to Joan and tell her that I often think about the good old times and hope that she can still remember the tall young man she called King Pole.'

Pat Pinder (18 July 2007)

'Circus Rosaire visited Bridlington each summer in the 1950s, they were in a field next to Postills Riding School in Fortyfoot. It was owned by Zena, Ted Bunning and their daughter Joan with her wonder horse Goldy. Dennis Rosaire, his Spanish wife Amelia and their two children Carmen and Carlos also helped out. I remember them having a parade through the town. My father was a big circus fan and went up there most nights, sometimes helping with jobs such as spotlights, selling ices etc.'

Bob North - (15 August 2007)

'I certainly remember Circus Rosaire as Postill's Field was just over the fence at the bottom of our garden where I still live. I remember Joan Rosaire, a daughter of the owners, who presented a brilliant act with horses she was also on TV. She was a lovely good-looking girl and very polite. She came over our fence one day to ask my late wife if she could have use of our bathroom. My son Bob and daughter Josie were aged approximately 10 and 12 years old at the time and got to speak to some of the performers, including the ringmaster and lion tamer by the name of Jim Parsons. He featured an act with lions and lionesses in his smart red outfit and sleek black hair. I remember after one performance he had to have one of his arms bandaged up, having been caught by one of the animal's claws. I also remember at certain times the local fire brigade fitting a hosepipe to a water hydrant to cool the animals down.'

A special joke we could hear over the tannoy just before every performance when someone would shout 'Is this the Follies?' The answer from the ring came back: 'No, it's Circus Rosaire, how did you get in?' – 'I came in on my brother's ticket' – 'Well, where's your brother?'- 'He's looking for his ticket mister.'

Joan remembers dear old Brid well with great affection and that she had made many good friends there and had passed her HGV driving test in Bridlington, allowing her to drive an HGV. Joan was 21 at the time and had been driving illegally for at least six year but soon after she passed her test she was stopped by a young policeman who was a little suspicious because he had not seen a woman before driving a large lorry. It was in the previous year while performing at Chessington Zoo in 1953 that Joan passed her basic driving test and bought her first car. The car was a 1932 sixteen horsepower Wolsey. It looked like something Al Capone might have driven.

Joan on Parade

Joan and Goldy at Bridlington - 1953

The battery was always flat but as Joan says: 'there was always a good crowd who were always willing to give a push to get it going.'

She also remembers the fun she had with either the other young members of the circus or those from the local area. One occasion she remembers well was when a group of them were running around the circus late one evening when she fell in the elephants' cess pool, getting hosed down and creeping back into her parents' caravan with the dog barking and her father asking where she had been. On another occasion another circus friend John Pugh lifted Joan up and dumped her in a horse's trough.

'They were great days and as my mother was not always around I even learned to cook. Previously that was her department, whilst I spent the entire time looking after and cleaning the horses, an occupation that has lasted a life time. It was a very happy period of my growing up.'

It was in the early 1950s when Joan's parents bought the bungalow 'Melbourne' next to the farm. Joan remembers the occasion well. 'I was in the field next to the bungalow exercising my horse John Wellington Wales (Johnny) a pure- bred bay Arab

Stallion when the neighbours over the hedge called me over, explaining that they were moving to the West Country and would the family like to buy it. I immediately called my father and we pooled all our savings and purchased it that afternoon for £2500. Structurally it was in a very bad condition, I mean very bad and it took my father many months to bring it up to an acceptable standard which included underpinning.'

Cecily Shufflebottom (nee Ross) already owned a bungalow next door 'Daisy Field ' and had done so since the late 1940s, she later sold it to her daughter Cicily and her husband Derek Owles for £300 plus Mink coat, the coat being worth more than the £300. Susan the daughter of Cicily and Joan's second cousin still lives in it today with her husband Ralph Bibby.

Joan and Gaye at Bridlington

Following Joan's grandfather's (the Count) death in November 1949 her parents along with Dennis Rosaire, took over the running of the circus, with Joan taking sole charge of the horses and other animals. Joan goes on to explain her dilemma: 'Life was no longer just fun but the welfare of our stock became deadly serious. The decisions that had to be made were now mine. Quite a lot of our horses were not in fact actual workers, a few pensioners and some just on "social security." We couldn't carry them all and it was down to me to decide which ones to keep and which ones to let go – a very difficult decision indeed.

In and around Billericay, I had many good friends. Quite a few were happy to relieve me of my burden. So, some of the ponies were rehabilitated as riding ponies and some just used as companions. Years later many were still around and I used to go and visit them.'

Joan and Gaye at their Dressing rooms at Chessington.

During the early 1950s before television really got a hold, circuses received a considerable amount of media press and Circus Rosaire was one and while they were performing at the Harringay Stadium, journalist Edward Graves with the World's Fair newspaper had this to say about Joan: -

'All-Too Brief Ballerina:

There is another young performer on this circus who gives evidence of sound tuition and personal appreciation of the advantages of making nice things even nicer by doing them correctly. She is Joan the shapely daughter of Zena and Ted Bunning, who has been making some surprise appearances on television. Her contributions to the Rosaire programme are numerous but the one which appeals to me is her bareback "Ballerina". It pleases and then arouses in me a feeling of disappointment as I told her, not for the first time and I repeat here.

What Joan pleases to show the audience of her talents in this degree of circus equestrian is delightful: toes point where toes should; body and limbs are poised in that style which assures grace; then movements are attractive and correctly timed. But there isn't enough of it. If a full three or four phase trick ride were beyond her capabilities then there would be nothing more to say but she can do the sequences she omits, evident in the comparatively little audiences are permitted to see. Indeed, a tantalising young woman. (Reproduced by kind permission of the World's Fair)'

Joan practicing her ballerina act on Vichy

Joan practised her Trick Riding/Ballerina act on Vichy at Billericay. The act comprised of ballerina movements and some daring trick riding movements such as skipping on the back of the horse, the act also included the horse going under a rope of streamers and Joan jumping over the rope and landing back on the horse – scary.

Joan in her Ballerina outfit

Joan being wooed by clown Rabbit at Chessington Zoo, with 'Vichy' in the background.

The World's Fair newspaper had been established in 1904 around the time Circus Rosaire started. It reports on funfairs, fairground events, business information and social events of travelling show people and the funfair industry. It remains one of the primary sources of information for showmen throughout the UK and their circus section features circus and show reviews, interviews with circus artistes and other circus professionals, regulations and other news affecting the circus industry.

Boxing Day 1954 saw the circus at the Royal Hippodrome, Eastbourne and though thick coconut matting on stage replaced the sawdust of the circus ring and the ring was reduced to only half the size of the 'big top,' the acts still captured the true circus atmosphere. On this occasion making her first professional appearance was 16 year old Carmen Rosaire, who under the name 'Miss Carmencita,' astounded the audience by her adventures on the trapeze.

Joan and her perfectly-schooled horses which no doubt included Goldy amongst them were as much at home on the coconut matting as if they had been on sawdust.

In 1955 Joan and Cousin Dennis Rosaire and his daughter Carmen found themselves in the film 'Women for Joe', it was a British drama film starring Diane Cilento, George Baker, Jimmy Karoubi and David Kossoff. The film was about the owner of a circus sideshow and his prize attraction a midget who both became romantically involved with the same woman. The highlight of this picture is the elaborate circus set and the majority of the acts were carried out by members of the Rosaire family. Dennis played the part of Franz with his knife throwing act and Joan being his assistant standing at the board being the target. Carmen was the midget stand-in for several of the flying trapeze performances and Joan also had her horses in the show. It was a Rank Organization production and filmed at Pinewood Studios.

Gaye enjoyed her time with Rosaires and as she says: - 'I was treated as one of the family but by the late 1950s work was becoming rather scarce due to the Television and the dreaded animal protesters so the family went off the road with the family slowly breaking up and going their own way. So, I decided it was time for me to move on and go out into the World to find another job, get married and have a family. Joan like the rest of the family went out on her own with the wonderful horse Goldy and what an institution they became.'

When Circus Rosaire closed for the last time (1956) it was a sad day for Joan. Although she had performed in many other circuses and theatres, her heart was with Circus Rosaire. She was only 23 and her career was just beginning, luckily she and Goldy were in great demand. Joan like a number of the Rosaire family decided in between working with the family circus to seek fresh fields and this stood her in good stead when the circus finally closed.

It was around 1957 just around the time that Gaye moved on that another young eight-year-old girl 'Jana' appeared on the scene. Her father Albert Kean was a circus clown but also trained and performed with all kinds of animals – Lions, Bears, Elephants, Ponies, Dogs, Monkeys, and Geese etc. Before coming to England he had his own circus in Belgium – 'Albert Kean Mini Circus'. Albert worked with the Sandows Circus during the 1940s and for a short time in the early 1950s for the Rosaires. It was, while with the Rosaires that the family decided that Jana needed some settled education and the Rosaires were more than happy for them to move and live in their caravan at the farm in Billericay.

Jana soon got into the swing of things and spent all her time when not at school helping Joan out. Looking after the horses, cleaning out the stables and as she got older helping out with the riding school and the local gymkhana shows. Jana went to Crays Hill School, then on to Billericay school and finally Timberlog School at Pitsea when the family eventually moved away from the farm. During the family's time at the farm, Albert was often away plying his trade in various circuses and theatres in England.

Jana enjoyed her time on the farm and though she moved on when she left school at fifteen has kept in regular contact with Joan. Jana's children today still refer to Joan as aunt. Jana did however return for one final show in 1979 at Burton on Trent when Joan was without a sidekick to help ride the horses.

Soon after Circus Rosaire closed down Joan got a telephone call from Derrick Rosaire who was in Switzerland with his horse 'Tony' working for Circus Knie. The horse was not very well so Derrick asked Joan if he could use Goldy. So, Joan on her own drove out to Switzerland with Goldy and worked for a time with Derrick.

This led in 1957 to Joan getting a contract to work in Spain for a season with Circo Americano. While out there a young man kept pestering Joan, she did not want anything to do with him, she complained to owners, who said they could do very little other than try and warn him off. Joan wrote to her mother about this young man and what a nuisance he was, a few days later Joan received a telegram from her mother to meet her grandmother 'Countess Rosaire' at the nearby airport, she was eighty at the time. The Countess soon put paid to the young man and spent the rest of the season in Spain and in North Africa travelling around with Joan. Unfortunately, while in Tangiers the Countess was robbed and had her purse stolen.

Then in 1958 Joan joined Derrick at Circus Knie. That year the circus was running a western theme for the whole of the second half of the programme. It started with a parade of horses, a chuck wagon and several other items. Lance King a Canadian singer and trick rider opened the show. Then Joan performed a cowboy voltige act on her ring horse 'Vichy' whom she had performed her ballerina number with in the first half. Derrick presented a comedy horse act with his horse Tony.

Joan's mother had flown Vichy out to Switzerland and when Joan arrived at the circus the first thing she did was to rush to the stables to see her. Vichy stood 15 hands and was almost pure white. Joan went right through the stables looking for her without success. Joan was getting a little upset but she had a little trick with Vichy. Joan would call her name and she would reply with a whinny. She called and to her amazement the reply came back not far from where Joan was standing. Vichy was tied up alongside one of the Lippizaner stallions. The stallion was behaving impeccably side by side with Vichy, a mare.

'I spent a very enjoyable season with Knie – a wonderful organisation, very correct, though things were very basic. Gas was difficult to obtain and knowing this, I had taken two huge cylinders from England when I went out to Spain, which with care had lasted me the season but were empty soon after arriving in

Switzerland. So, as they were taking up a lot of room, I decided to jettison them. On leaving one town, I left them behind. The next day a parcel arrived for me, special delivery – my gas bottles! Well after three abortive attempts, finally Herr Fredy Knie appeared at my wagon and asked, 'Rosaire' do you want these bloody bombs or not? They are costing me a fortune in carriage! Such was the thoroughness of their organisation that you couldn't even lose something if you wanted to!'

It was while travelling through the mountains in Switzerland that Joan had a scare when the brakes on her vehicle failed. Lance King was following behind. He took over Joan's vehicle and she drove his.

At one of the shows in the audience was Charlie Chaplin, Joan said she would like to meet him, Mr Knie invited her along to the reception wagon where she had dinner with him. During the evening she said she would like his autograph. Charlie Chaplin immediately picked up a post card and signed the back for her. She has it to this day.

Joan at KNIE Circus, Switzerland

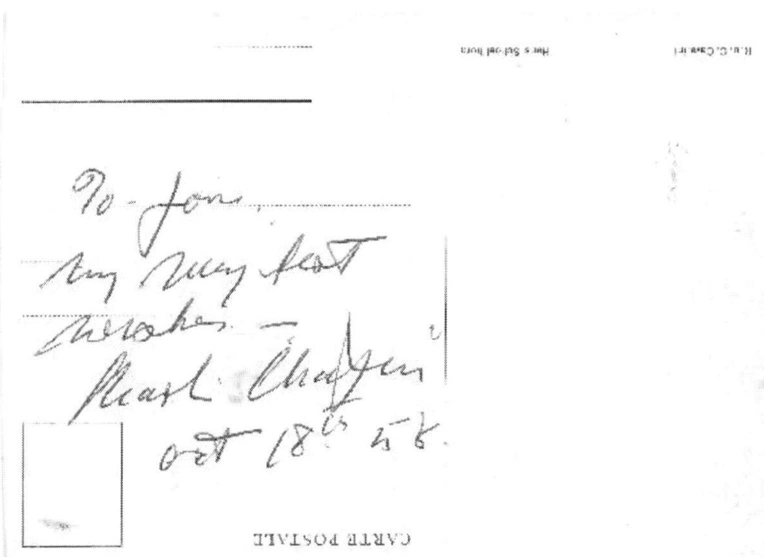

Post card signed by Charlie Chaplin

Joan working with Lance King on their Cowboy and Trick Riding act.

In 1959 back home in Billericay Joan decided to start up a riding school. Joan admits she knew very little about riding schools
and it was therefore a bit of a gamble but she knew she could teach people to ride. There was an occasion though when Joan was not feeling very well and Cousin David offered to take her riding group out but somehow, he managed to come back without them. That was the first and last time Joan allowed him to take a group out. Joan goes on to explain: 'We still had a few horses left from the circus, so we all had a career change! It was quite a lot of fun. I made a lot of friends and even ran my own gymkhanas. Mother did the catering for them and Dad built the show jumps – and very inventive they were. We had all kinds of competitions for the able – and for the less able, fancy dress, both horse and rider. Along with my riding school they became enormously popular.'

One gymkhana in September 1963 included five jumping events and seven gymkhana events. With the five jumping events were five trophies to be won: - Layland Challenge Cup, Willoughby Challenge Cup, Bunning Challenge Cup, Hill Trophy and Ward Trophy. The gymkhana events being a Hat Race (leading rein, children 9 years and under), Bending Race (open), Potato Race (children, 14 years and under), Sack Race (open), Dressing up Race (Children 16 years and under), Bareback Trotting (Open) and Musical Chairs (open). They were always well attended and Joan says 'everybody seemed to enjoy the afternoons.' Many locals remember their time at the riding school learning to ride.

Patsy Birch - Billericay Community Archive (29 November 2012) – 'I met Joan when I was a little girl, she taught me how to ride a horse the right way, never forget her, wonderful horse women. Xx.'

Joan was also quite happy to go along to local schools, one such occasion was the sports day at Dunton County Primary School, Lower Dunton Road, Dunton. The following is just one of the many letters received from the school expressing their enjoyment of the performance and seeing Goldy.

Poster

Outside Event with Silver

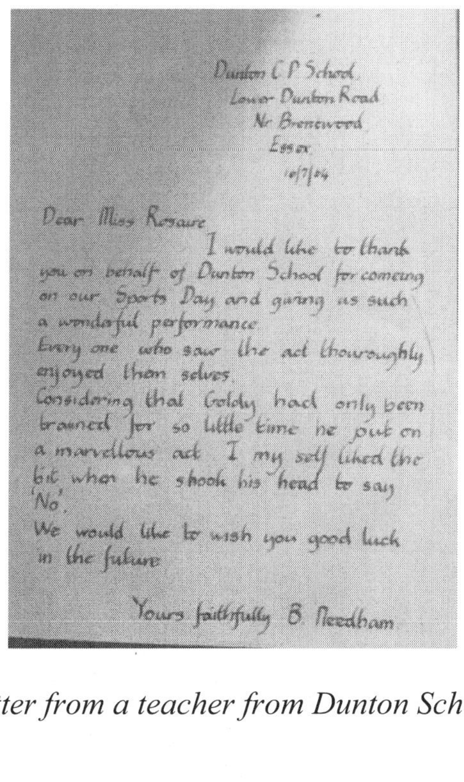

Dunton C P School,
Lower Dunton Road
Nr Brentwood
Essex
10/7/84

Dear Miss Rosaure
I would like to thank you on behalf of Dunton School for coming on our Sports Day and giving us such a wonderful performance
Every one who saw the act thouroughly enjoyed them selves.
Considering that Goldy had only been trained for so little time he put on a marvellous act. I my self liked the bit when he shook his head to say 'No'.
We would like to wish you good luck in the future

Yours faithfully B. Needham

Letter from a teacher from Dunton School

Local school sports days must have been a speciality of Joan's because we also find her at a Billericay Sports day signing autographs.

Joan signing autographs at Billericay School

There were times however, when Joan became short of money, the first time in the early 1960s she found herself a job in a local apple packing factory. Then on another occasion in the 1970s she went to work as a receptionist for a local doctor. He wanted to train her up to do more but she was unable to fit the training around her circus work. On another occasion Joan was offered a job as a TV announcer but again turned it down because of her commitment to her horses.

It was also around the early 1960s that Joan started to become allergic to horses, in fact the headline in the Daily Mirror in January 1972 read:-

Nose for Trouble

Spare a thought this morning for Joan Rosaire who does an act in Billy Smart's Circus (currently at Croydon) with a palomino horse called Goldy. She is allergic to horses. 'It is something that started eight years ago and is getting worse.'

Another outside event – Orsett, July 1964

Although she was going to suffer for the rest of her life there was no way it was going to stop her performing. In a report by the local Evening Echo in June 1986 she admits that when she is around horses for any length of time she gets quite asthmatic. Not that any of the audiences noticed that she is suffering as Goldy, laughs, counts, dances and rears up, jumping into the air with all the bounce of Zebedee.

The call of the circus however was too great and stimulated by the birth of Goldy's foal (Goldy's Boy), a lively youngster who promised to be an even better performer than her mother, So Joan in 1965 went back into the circus business. She joined Robert Brothers' Circus for a short tenting tour, then it was off for a season with them at the Great Yarmouth Hippodrome where she presented an exotic animal act which included a giant camel, a bull, a llama, a zebra and a donkey plus a troupe of coloured horses.

Goldy and Goldy's Boy

Unfortunately, the bull used to mess on the stage and on one occasion one of the animals slipped over. Joan came to the rescue by getting the various helpers to take all the animals away from the bull just before the acts which then got it very apprehensive and resulting in it messing. She would then go on with the act with no further mishaps. As Joan says, 'it's all about knowing your animals.'

Just before going to Yarmouth Goldy died in Joan's arms in the stable so it was Goldy's boy that went with her and she was able to practise with him in her spare time.

Barbara Bethel - Billericay Community Archive (8 February 2016) – 'I remember Joan, she taught me and my sister (Patsy Potter) and Mother (Doris) to ride. I also remember Goldy having a foal. No one knew she was expecting and were most surprised, they called it Goldy's Boy.'

Joan with Goldy's Boy.

This came about by Joan becoming friendly with another well-known Laindon celebrity 'Billy Foyle' and his beautiful palomino horse 'King'. Billy like Joan had taught King to do many tricks, his favourite was to play football. You can see the horse on British Pathe news kicking a football then going into the bar at the Laindon Hotel, Laindon for a pint. Billy was often seen dressed as a Wild West Marshall on King at the Basildon Carnivals in the 1950/60s. On the odd occasion Joan would accompany him on Goldy. Though it was these occasions that Joan was not too keen on showing Goldy off as she considered it too dangerous for the horse.

Billy set up home at Whitebridge Farm only a few miles away from Rosaire's winter quarters. He had opened up there a small zoo which included at times, bears, llamas, camels, monkeys, lions and tigers and of course we must not forget his horses. It was Billy who persuaded Joan to let 'King' sire Goldy.

Joan was a little concerned because Goldy was over twenty at the time but as we know it turned out okay and Goldy's Boy was born. Goldy's Boy was the only one she bred herself.

Billy Foyle and King

As Billy had his own small zoo he was able to supply the circus with animal food, in particular meat for the lions. Payment was not always in cash and on one occasion payment was made by giving Billy a horsebox that Joan's father had built.

There was an occasion, although quite amusing, that could have been very serious and this was when four of Joan's horses escaped from a field where they were grazing. Joan had rented a good grazing field in the Ramsden Crays area some two/three miles away. She would ride Goldy leading Goldy's Boy and two other horses along the road to the field and leave them there to graze. Goldy would have other ideas and on at least two occasions unhooked the gate and led the horse's home along the grass verge. As Joan says 'Goldy was a clever devil and we had to have strong locks put on the gate to stop any further recurrences.'

In 1964 just as Jana was moving on Joan met Tracy who was eight at the time and like Gaye and Jana was going to become her close companion for the next fifteen years, but her opening words to her were 'Bugger off' but that was our Joan very strict and protective of her horses – it was going to be a comment that always amused Tracy. Tracy had been enthralled by watching a circus on the television, it was the animals that excited her the most, in particular Joan and her wonder horse Goldy. She had learnt to ride at Brook Farm Riding School, Billericay, so like Joan she had caught the horse bug early and as she only lived a couple of miles away from Willoughby Farm she used to cycle to the farm, stand by the white paddock rails to wait and see the lovely Goldy. The rebuke came on an occasion that Goldy had come close enough for Tracy to pat her. Little Tracy got a telling off and told to leave the horses alone. This did not deter her and she kept coming back to watch from afar. Joan eventually said if you must hang around come on in and you can learn to muck out. This was the start of another long partnership and friendship.

Tracy first helped Joan's father muck out the pigs for 50p but eventually Joan let her help out with the horses. A year or so later Tracy's parents bought her a pony call 'Jinks' (Bay Mare) she was a bit of a devil so Joan had her stay on the farm for a week and retrained her, she was fine after that and as Tracy says Joan knew her horses. Jinks was kept on Watts Farm, South Green so Tracy was either at Watts Farm or at Joan's. Tracy takes up the story:-

'After ten months of bliss owning a pony, I found her laying in the field killed by overhead wires that had come down in the wind which ran across the field. The following day Joan asked me to come to the farm and do some training with a small Palomino stallion she had by the name of 'Weasel'. He was a bit of a devil so Joan had him gelded, this calmed him down and after some more training my parents bought him for me. Soon after this I started to help Joan exercise her Arab Stallion "Johnny" he was a fantastic horse – a real gent.'

Joan mucking out

'Whilst still at Junior School (Sunnymead, Outwood Common) Joan used to meet me half way home, she would be riding Johnny and leading Goldy's Boy. I would put one foot in Joan's left stirrup and she would haul me up by the scruff of the neck and I would ride Goldy bare back, hanging on to a neck strap for dear life. Joan would drop me off at home.'

'For the next seven years when not at school my days were full helping the family and Joan mucking out the pigs, horses and riding the horses. I hated school and school hated me all I wanted to do was be with the horses so on leaving school my parents allowed me to move in with Joan and her family. Joan's mother Zena was a lovely lady but now a retired circus artist and animal trainer. Joan's father was a very clever man, coachbuilder, farmer, he could turn his hand to about everything. I learnt a lot from him such as how to be practical, drive the tractor bring in the hay and how to sign write.

Art was becoming my second love and I learnt to design and paint fairground art. While Joan was away overseas, I would look after the horses left behind and her father following the passing of Joan's dear mother.'

John Wellington Wells (Johnny) going through his paces.

It was in 1965 that Bobby Roberts of Roberts Bro's circus asked her to take his liberty horses and exotics to Great Yarmouth for the season. The horses were a very nice troupe of black and whites that did a smart and intricate routine. The problem was if you happened to be in the wrong place you had a good chance of being run over.

Joan also had her moments with the exotics: one camel called Jordan, bull named Ferdy, a llama and zebra but the one animal that really caused her problems was David the donkey. He had the habit of finding ways of getting out of doing his routine and it became a battle of wits. He gave Joan a lifelong aversion to donkeys.

Goldy with Joan at Yarmouth

It was in August 1965 whilst at Yarmouth Joan made her first television appearance with the new Goldy. A local evening paper reported that the accent of the televised show by the B.B.C. would be on the girls and one such girl was Joan Rosaire who in her short career to date had been a trapeze walker, trampoline specialist and now a presenter of animal acts, in particular horses.

Following this T.V. appearance she was chosen to represent 'The Circus' in the Grand Parade of Working Horses at the Horse of the Year Show at Wembley. So pleased were the organisers of this show by the appearance of Goldy that Joan was presented by Colonel Sir Michael Ansell, the Chairman, with a golden horseshow bracelet. This was the first of many television appearances including several television advertisements.

Goldy's Boy as a unicorn in Dr Who

One such was when in the late 1960s they appeared in the Rediffusion children's program 'Hullabaloo' and following soon afterwards Goldy's Boy appeared as a unicorn in Dr Who, as Joan says 'he only does character acts, not bit parts.' Joan believed he really enjoyed the part; it was filmed at the dead of night on a disused aerodrome. Goldy Boy was chosen for the part because he was just about the only horse in the country who could perform without a bridle. As Joan explains take the bridle off most horses and the last thing, you'll see is its tail streaming off into the horizon. In the part Goldy's Boy had to appear in the distance, rear up and come charging down on Dr Who and like the real professional he was he did everything asked of him without knocking over any of the actors. The Doctor was Patrick Troughton the Second Doctor, the episode 'Land of Fiction.'

Joan was back at Yarmouth in 1966 but this time it was with her own horse act with Goldy. Following these two Yarmouth outings it stood Joan in good stead when presenting 16 liberties for Bouglione in later years.

It was during the 1960s that Joan met Princess Margaret and her children. It was on an occasion when she was performing for Smarts Circus. The Princess and the children wanted to see the horses so before the show started, Joan arranged for them to come back stage for tea and cake and to see the horses, Goldy in particular.

Joan initially got involved with the Essex Union Hunt, in Kennel Lane, Billericay by going along and helping Reg Brooks the stable man clip the horses. It took up to one and a half hours to clip a horse. Joan used to turn the handle of the clipping machine while Reg ran the clipper over the horse. It was from the Essex Union Kennels whom she purchased a seven-week-old foal, naming it Trampus.

Although she would often appear at the start of an Essex Union Hunt, she never actually joined in as she believed it was too dangerous for her precious horses. However, she occasionally performed at their annual balls.

Trampus, Joan believes was the most talented of her horses though he was not as trustworthy as the others in fact as Joan explains he was a bit of a juvenile delinquent.

Joan in her riding gear (Essex Union Hunt)

Joan performing at the Essex Union Ball

For example, Silver would stand by her obediently even at prestige events such as Olympia but Trampus would get a little restless and want to wander off to investigate his surroundings. Saying that, they all kiss her on command, bow at the knee, open gates and ring out dainty horseshow tap dances of dressage. They always looked magnificent with their glowing dun-coloured coats and pale silk-yellow manes and tails.

You needed to watch these wonderful animals at the farm as Joan unlocked their stalls. Good locks were needed, anything else they found easy to open. Joan would then lead them into the lungeing arena and you would have marvelled at the intensity of their bond with her.

Perhaps her deepest bond was with Silver. Silver would curl his neck round Joan's, give her a long-toothed grin and ask for advance payment in the form of mints. He would then prove how laid back he is by nonchalantly crossing his legs. If you were lucky you would then see Duke, snorting with joy as he unlocks the gate to the lungeing arena with his nose and with payment of a mint from Joan would then set off on a Spanish walk with his proud leg lift from the shoulder rather than the knee. It is then you might just see some slight movements by Joan, like the twitching of her shoulder from which the horses obey her immediately.

As you would have gathered Joan had several Goldys, the original, Goldy's Boy, followed by 'Silver' who she bought from a scrapyard in Ramsden Heath for £125. Silver was going to be one of the most talented. It all came about by Joan and her father visiting the breakers yard with her father looking for a part for her horsebox. She asked the dealer if he dealt in second-hand horse s as well. 'Yes came the reply and I do part exchange.' Well it did not take long for Joan to purchase a scruffy-looking yearling colt but she promptly left it with her mother as she went off on her circus travels again. On her return he had grown into a 'handsome lad' standing 15.2 hands high, with a gorgeous golden colouring. He was not the easiest of horses to train but Joan was very proud of him and he performed superbly in public from day one and went on to do so until his retirement with laminitis at the age of 22.

Then came 'Duke' who she bought off a lady for £1000 who was going off to Australia but could not afford to take him with her. Trampus followed and finally she purchased Sunny off Geoff (Jeff) Winship. Although her horses had their individual names when they performed, they performed under the name of Goldy. Jeff was born and raised in a circus, spending his time as an acrobat, a trapeze artist, a clown and trick rider but he found his vocation as the 'Black Knight' on account of the role he played in the world's only touring mediaeval jousting tournament.

It was not only British Television she appeared on, in 1967 she appeared in the French Television Show 'La Piste aux Etoiles' filmed at Cirque d'Hiver in Paris. Joan always goes on about her lack of education so suggest you look at the performance on You Tube, her French is not bad! Nor is her German come to that.

Joan left on Silver and Tracy on Duke

It was only Goldy's Boy only second performance. As previous mentioned the Bougliones family owners of Cirque d'Hiver were so pleased with Joan that she was invited to present their sixteen-strong liberty horse act for a season and anyone who knows how highly the Bougliones regard their horse presentation will know that this was a high honour indeed.

Just prior to her first performance at the circus, Joan a day or so before had turned up to the circus to familiarize herself with it but found nobody there other than a man in a white overall. She followed him around all day, making the odd drink, communication was limited because he only spoke French and Joan at the time could only speak English. Towards the end of the day he tried to get rid of her but Joan wanted to go into a particular room, eventually he gave way and showed her in. 'It was the Gentleman's'.

At this time the Bougliones were scheduled to do a TV advert on French Television but all their wagons were being serviced. So Joan gave them her wagon for the advert. As she says:-'we in the circus business just help each other out.'

It was also around this time that doing a ballerina act riding bareback Joan fell off, injuring her leg. Joan said 'it was a nerve –racking act. Every time I used to go into the ring I'd wonder if I would be brought out on a stretcher.' So as one would expect she gave up this part of her circus repertoire.

As well as with horses Joan also as we know built up a great rapport with any animals that came her way, we have already mentioned Billy the llama and by now she had also been training dogs and befriending lion cubs etc. Another example was her training of the circus geese to slide, jump through a hole and walk under a tunnel. There was however one goose that she had to keep an eye on who her grandfather, like the llama, had brought home from a pub. The goose became his protector and behold anybody that got to close to him when he was around. On the day of grandfather's funeral, he followed the funeral possession out of the farm until Dennis Rosaire managed to coax it away then after that he became Dennis's protector.

In August 1968 Robert Fossett, the well-known circus impresario assembled in Rhyl top circus stars to take part in his summer season 'The Big Top Continental Circus' at the pavilion. Igor Gridneff set the scene as ringmaster, there were the clowns, aerial acrobatics, full grown rock python, hypnotised crocodiles, poodles and of course there was Joan with her Shetland ponies and 'Goldy-Wonder Horse' providing the equine flair.

Then with Chipperfield's at Leamington in April 1969 a mongrel puppy was found abandoned at the circus camp by Peter the clown and as Joan was the only person at the circus without a dog he moved in with her. As we know Joan and Goldy shared the same caravan and Goldy usually did not like dogs because one had bitten him previously but surprisingly, they both got on very well.

Chippy and Joan

When it was time for the circus to move on to its next venue which in fact was to the Cattle Market at Rugby, Joan had no option but to take Chippy with her but Chippy was having to earn his keep. Joan trained him and future dogs she was to have. She taught them to jump, walk on their hind legs, skip etc. To skip she used to have the rope held up just a few feet away from a wall so when the dog jumped over the rope it could not run away, then with a little bit of fuss it did not take them long to master this routine and go into the ring and perform for Joan. She also trained her dogs to sing along with her when she sang 'How much is that doggy in the window' they would bark at the appropriate place.

In August 1970 Joan appeared at the Pavilion, Rhyl with the 'Big Top Circus' and this is what the local papers had to say – 'While the animal acts are few this year, the quality and artistic presentation remains as high as ever, and the delight they give, particularly to the young members is obvious. Joan Rosaire provides traditional circus atmosphere with her Liberty horses and Goldy, an almost human horse which has been featured on television.'

Joan with Goldy at the Big Top Circus, Rhyl two years earlier in 1968

During the early years of the 1970s Joan also found herself working one of the summer seasons at Blackpool Tower Circus. She invited Tracy up for a two weeks holiday. Tracy takes up the story: - 'The Tower is the most fantastic place. The Circus, the ballroom, the stables were all underground. Seeing all the glamour and glitz behind the scenes was amazing such an honour. There was a riding act "Jimmy, Jerry, and Johnny" and on one occasion while the performers were practising with them they invited Joan to trick ride their horse "Lonny." I had never seen Joan perform this act before as she had stopped sometime back due to wear and tear on her knees, in fact she had had an operation on one. Trick riding is very risky and I was pleased to see a side of Joan's amazing repertoire that I had not seen before.'

Between performances the horses were stabled just outside Blackpool and Tracy stayed with Joan in the cottage on wheels with Tracy sleeping on a sun bed in the horse part. On one occasion when both Joan and Tracy were out exercising Johnny and Goldy. Goldy stood on Tracy's right foot, swivelled round and tore off her big toenail. Needless to say it hurt but she continued with the daily exercise but when she eventually took her boot off there was blood everywhere – not a pretty sight.

Sometime during the mid-1970s, Joan had an invite to appear at Chipperfield Circus at Bingly Hall, Birmingham to perform a highwayman act. Both Joan and Tracy set off in the cottage, fully laden with Goldy's Boy, Johnny and Silver, costumes, tack, hay and the living quarters consisting of two bunk beds, cooker, heater and the kitchen sink. On arrival the horses were set up in nearby stables, horsebox secured all appeared well. Next day Joan was working with Silver and Tracy was grooming Johnny when she noticed that Goldy's Boy was laying down and not looking well. Tracy ran and got Joan, shouting that she thought Goldy's Boy had colic, a vet was soon in attendance and confirmed that he did have colic. He gave him some pain killers. Joan in the meantime had to get young Silver ready to take over the act that evening, it was also Tracy's first time in the ring. Joan had made all the costumes for the act – black cornered hats with white fluffy feathers around the top of the hat, fitted purple jackets, white riding trousers and black boots to the knees. Joan would ride into the ring on 'Silver' followed by Tracy on 'Johnny' they would perform a high school routine and Tracy would leave Joan on her own to continue with the rest of the act.

In between the performances Joan and Tracy walked Goldy's Boy to keep him on his feet. For two days and nights they both sat and walked with him and other performers helped out. The vet came every day but it was soon clear that Goldy's Boy had had enough, his gut had twisted so as Joan says, 'although I loved my horses I could not see him suffer so I reluctantly agreed to have him put down.' As you would expect everybody in the show was terribly upset and Joan was devastated. Her second Goldy had gone. As we know he was the one horse she was to breed from a mare which meant that they had a real close bond though he could be a bit of a devil and very seldom tolerated other people.

Following the season at Bingley Hall it was back to Billericay and the daily routine of mucking out, training the younger horses, haymaking etc.

Then there was a short season in Britain with the Chipperfields followed by going on tour with Jeff Windships, Cowboy Rodeo Show which took both Joan and Tracy all over the U.K. Joan was not involved in the cowboy acts - she and Goldy performed their own act. Joan followed this up with an invite for a season at Yarmouth Circus but on this occasion, Tracy stayed behind to look after the hay making, mucking out, the house and looking after Joan's father.

There followed a short winter season at Kelvin Halls, Glasgow. The horsebox was parked inside the hall as there was a very large fair set up outside. The fairground noise was so loud that by the end of the evening Joan and Tracy's ears would ring for hours after. As Joan says it was very difficult to concentrate. The large circus ring was purpose built adjoining the hall with a balcony for the band. The local papers reported that Joan Rosaire makes her Golden Horses and especially Goldy the Wonder Horse assisted by Miss Tracy, do most things but talk.

Joan Haymaking

Joan with Goldy then went off on their own to do a show at a large night club in Holland for a few days. With her was Cousin David and his dog act and Michael Austin and his 101 Tumbler act. During the late 1950s and early 1960s, Joan, David and Michael were inseparable. Michael though not part of the family lived for a time at Wilborough Farm. His father Charlie was a famous circus clown but though Michael stayed in the circus world he concentrated on trapeze, bareback riding etc. He remembers Joan on at least one occasion cutting his hair with horse clippers.

Just after finishing a season at the Tower Circus, Joan's agent sent her a booking to appear at a theatre in Brighton. This meant driving down in the horsebox, keeping the horse in the box and living with him. The horse she took on this occasion was Johnny. It was an exhausting but pleasurable trip but, on her return, Tracy back home in Billericay was extremely relieved to see her. Joan discovered her in the stable cleaning out the stalls with a pitchfork tied to a broom. 'What's going on here? Joan asked, it's him she said, he won't let me near him when you are not here. I don't think he likes me.' The horse was Silver, who could at times be a little naughty, when Joan was not around he thinks he is in charge.

Over time Joan had several horseboxes/caravans built on the chassis of Lorries by her father for her and horses to travel in and as you would have gathered they often referred to them as a 'cottage on wheels' where her sleeping compartment had a communicating door through which the two could talk to each other. Joan goes on to explain: - 'Goldy had his own bedroom in the caravan because after such an act as ours, I just cannot walk away and forget him. To get the best out of an animal you must know its reactions and I am a bit of a nut anyway. We talked to each other and he always came shopping with me at home. He was no trouble but he did make a bit of a noise when he turned over at night.'

Joan later appeared with Billy Smart's at Croydon's Fairfield Halls with summers and winters with Chipperfields; two seasons at Blackpool Tower; two at Great Yarmouth Hippodrome and two at the Pavilion, Rhyl; Circo Americano in Spain, Cirque d'Hiver in Paris, the Coliseo, Porto and many leading cabarets. Joan had by now become nationally or even internationally known as a great horsewoman and was invited with her horses to take part at the Theatre Royal, Drury Lane in the musical spectacular 'Gone with the Wind', starring June Richie and Harve Presnell.

Her horse had to look hungry and so old that it's about to drop. Goldy would have been no good for this part so she purchased two new horses, one called 'Charlie' who fitted the bill perfectly and a large Bay Mare called Nellie to act as Charlie's understudy.

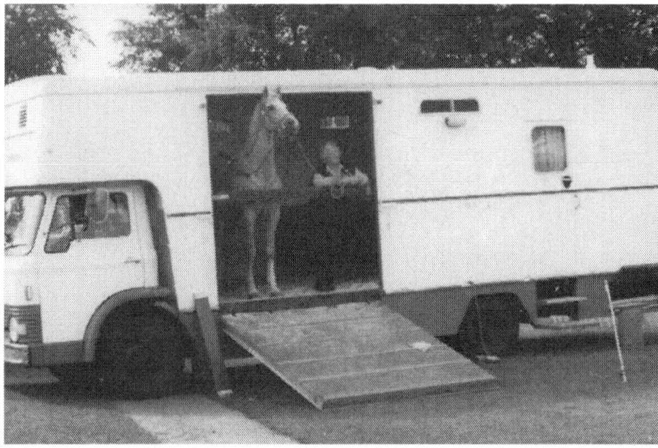

Just one of Joan's many Horsebox/Caravans that her dad built (Trampas)

Joan with her third Goldy, 'Silver'

Back at the farm and after a couple of days settling in Joan borrowed from Tracy her coster four wheeled trolley to start their training for the show. Charlie had pulled a cart before so Joan hitched up Nellie to Tracy's trolley and at a later date to a cart that Joan's father had built for the act. Nellie was not quite as obedient as Charlie and on one occasion Tracy had hitched Nellie up to the two wheeled cart with Joan sitting in the cart holding the reins. As Joan asked Nellie to go forward the horse had other ideas and gave a very large buck. The cart straps that held the cart shafts in place broke, the shafts shot up in the air the cart tipped backwards and Joan shot out onto the ground. Tracy grabbed the horse's left rein and found herself flying around in circles. Joan as she was getting up shouted "don't let her go," and as Tracy hung on Joan managed to get hold of the reins and calm Nellie down. Nellie was a heavy Irish mare and Tracy was barely nine stone, a frightening experience but all ended well with surprisingly no injuries other than Joan with a sore bottom.

The horses were trained to walk forward, stop and run on the spot. Charlie was very good but though Nellie could do the same she would also half rear and hop on one back leg, which actually looked amazing but not really part of the act. In one exciting scene representing the Great Fire of Atlanta City Charlie had to run on the spot. He was given special boots otherwise he would have slipped over on the stage floor.

In another scene he would be led to the front of the cart by Tracy who was dressed as a soldier, she would hitch up and Joan also dressed as a soldier sitting in the cart holding the reins would drive Charlie forward, then stop and on command by Joan the horse would run on the spot, from the front of the stage it appeared as if the horse was running. Tracy would also be next to the horse also running on the spot with the command 'up Charlie' which he did before they exited the stage. It was not long before Charlie would go to the front of the cart without any help. Joan beforehand would groom him and then make him look untidy.

Every day for a year Joan or her mother would be at every performance.

Charlie and the Fire

This is what they had to say in the programme: -'*Almost as difficult as the human casting was the problem of finding a horse to take Scarlett and Melanie out of the burning Atlanta, home to the safety of Tara.*

The producers entrusted this tricky problem to an acknowledged equine expert, Joan Rosaire. Daughter, and granddaughter of circus folk, Miss Rosaire is famous throughout England and Europe as an animal trainer.

She bought two suitable horses (for even the horse must have an understudy), and began their training many months ahead of the scheduled opening so that both horses became fully accustomed to the noises and flame effects used in the Atlanta burning sequence.

As was only to be expected, the horses have become the darlings of the company and the major disciplinary problem backstage is to prevent the actors over-indulging them with loaf sugar.'

At one of the performances Princess Anne was in the audience and after the show went back stage to meet all the artists. Joan with little Charlie was at the end of the long line of artists being introduced to the Princess. Joan could see that she was in a hurry to get to her and the horse. When she reached them she commented 'I see he has got boots on', Joan replied that without the boots on he would not have been able to stand up or walk on the wooden floor. 'Good – very interesting' was the Princess's reply.

Joan had arranged stabling for Charlie and Nellie at nearby Whitbread stables, where they would be groomed and got ready before heading off on the short journey to Drury Lane. After the show Joan and Tracy would ride them back to the stables in the dark with lights on their stirrups. Unfortunately, on one occasion they had a little bit of trouble when coming up to some lights in Oxford Street when a group of troublemakers came running up, banging tin lids and grabbing Nellie's reins. They pulled so hard that Nellie fell over landing on Joan's left foot breaking it.

With the troublemakers gone Tracy went back to the stables with Charlie and returned with the stable man and a wheelbarrow, which they wheeled Joan back in. The stable man strapped the foot up before Joan drove home. The next day Joan drove the horsebox with Goldy aboard to do another show with Tracy having to do the Drury Lane Show.

There was another occasion when Joan came across the Princess and that was at a Gala at Windsor. Joan with Tracy and Goldy (Silver) were leaning on the rail across the ramp of the caravan, when over the brow of a hill the Princess came charging down on a horse calling it all the names possible in an attempt to control it and when she got close to Joan she heard her shout out 'you are a naughty boy'.

Joan, Tracy, Charlie and Nellie arrived at the stage door at the same time Harve had arrived in his car so he obliged with a photograph.

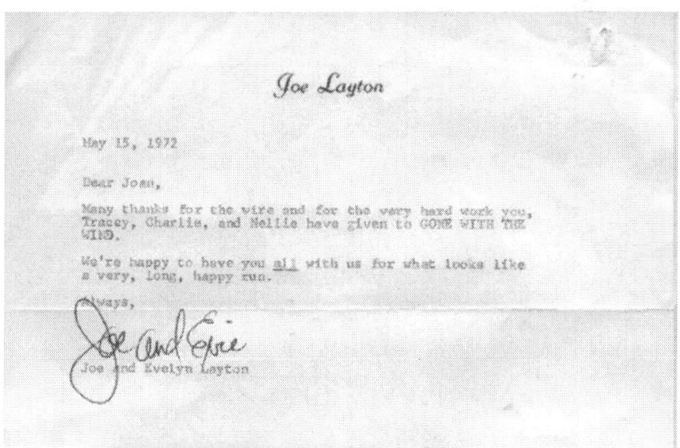

Joe Layton

May 15, 1972

Dear Joan,

Many thanks for the wire and for the very hard work you, Tracey, Charlie, and Nellie have given to GONE WITH THE WIND.

We're happy to have you all with us for what looks like a very, long, happy run.

Always,

Joe and Evie

Joe and Evelyn Layton

Joe Layton Directed and Choreographed the whole production.

While this show was going on Joan also accepted engagements at two other London Theatres, one being on the Max Bygraves singalong show at the Victoria Palace where Joan's horse would just stand pull a face and look away from the audience with Max Bygraves sitting on him. Joan made it clear to Max that she had to be in the wings as the horse would only work for her.

However, there was an occasion when Joan was not there and Cicily, Joan's cousin deputised for her. Max slapped Goldy with the reins on both sides of the neck like the cowboys do, surprisingly Max found himself on the floor. Max would not go near Joan for a few days and when he did Joan said 'I know what you did.' He did take her for a drink.

Max with Goldy

Jimmy Tarbuck took over from Max for a week to give him a break and though he knew Joan well decided not to use the horse in his act.

Jo Buckley the Features Editor of the magazine 'Lucky Rider' called on Joan and Goldy just prior to them going on stage:

'There I was, standing outside London's Victoria Palace Theatre – where the Max Bygraves Show is currently being staged – wondering whether a hand or a hoof would open the door to me. After all, I had been warned that Goldy is an extremely clever horse!

But it was Goldy's owner, Joan Rosaire, who opened the door to me. "Come in," she said, "I'm putting his shoes on!" And there, in his own private compartment of Miss Rosaire's horsebox-cum-caravan, I spied Goldy himself, a 14.2 hands high Palomino gelding, halfway between his darker winter colouring and his golden summer coat.

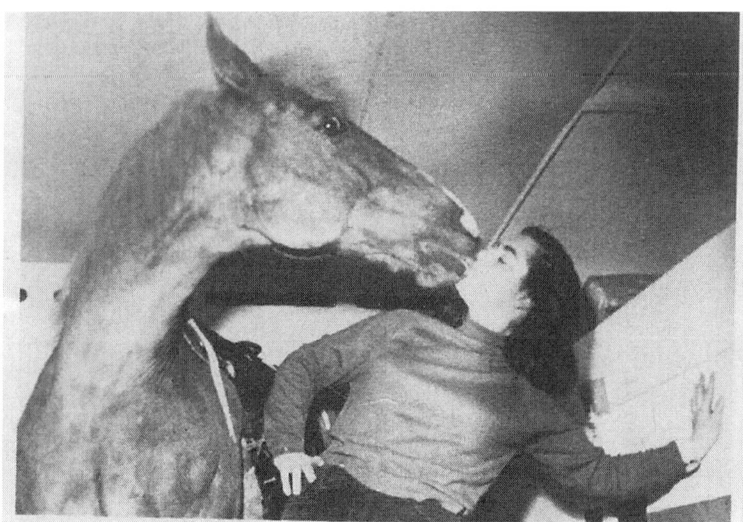

Goldy kissing Joan

He is a lovely animal, with huge, bright brown eyes and that superb creamy mane and tail that are characteristic of the breed. The very first thing he did when I entered his box was to kiss Miss Rosaire right on the nose after which he promptly turned round and gave me a big wet sloshy one too!.

Joan went on to explain that they are so attached to each other that if she goes out the horsebox for an hour or two she has to leave the radio on to keep him company, otherwise he just frets till she returns.

In the short time we had and in the limited space of the horsebox, Joan put him through a few of his paces for me. First of all they held a conversation, Joan asking him questions, whilst he mouthed replies, shook or nodded his head accordingly. Then he bent all four legs and rocked backwards and forwards like a rocking horse, crossed his legs, picked up his halter and even helped Joan on with her coat! On stage, of course, his act is a lot more complicated. In fact, he even plays football! What a Horse.'

In the third theatre Joan provided an old mare called 'Cristabell' for the pantomime Babes in the Wood at the London Palladium. Joan's cousin Cicily's husband Derek would drive the horse up to London daily from Billericay. The star of the panto was the comedian Julian Orchard and he would walk on sitting on the horse with a great flowing skirt on. Joan did not think much of that. Another sketch was the horse would walk on with a robber on its back and another would swing out of the trees and knock him off.

Three shows, three theatres and sometimes matinees as well which meant six shows a day in different locations and as you would expect there were frantic journeys across London often in the rush hours. The horses in a mad rush from one theatre to another soon learned how to work the traffic pads to change the lights.

The Panto and Goldy at Victoria Palace were short runs unlike Gone with the Wind that went on for a year. In between the matinee and evening show on a Wednesday Joan and Tracy would

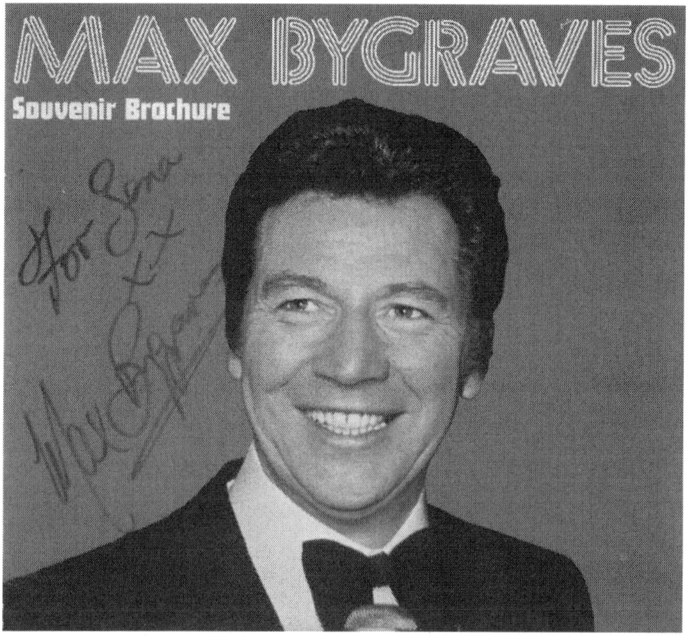

Before leaving the show, Joan made sure she got a signed brochure for her mother.

go and have some refreshments but on one of these occasions they returned to find Charlie lying on his bed in his stall, in real distress. He had broken one of his back legs and could not get up. Joan called a vet and while they were waiting for him to come all the staff backstage sat with him. Unfortunately, he had to be put down.

Though Joan was again very upset for losing another horse the show had to go on, so Nellie was prepared for the evening show. She had not been on stage for a while and it took a few shows before she really settled in. After the shows Tracy used to ride her back to the stables but Nellie was not one for walking and would set off at a pace, Joan would often drive past in a car shouting 'Slow her up.'

Unfortunately, with the death of little Charlie it meant she had to double with one horse for two of the theatres. Although it was a very exciting time for Joan, it was also a very worrying time as the IRA were carrying out a bombing campaign in London.

Eventually the show closed and Nellie was taken back to Billericay where Joan retired her and gave her to a friend. Later when Zena was ill in hospital with cancer, June Richie would visit her and spend a couple of hours, something that Joan has never forgotten.

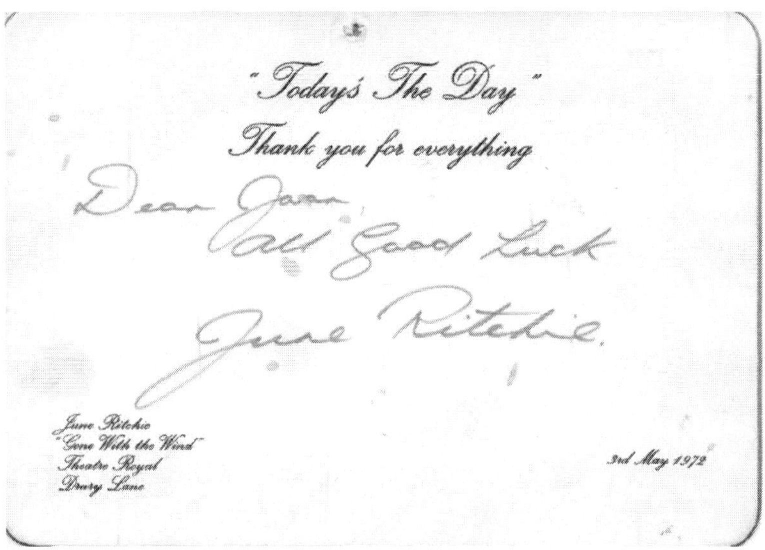

Thank you card from Joan Ritchie

Irene Heath, Journalist with Women's Weekly wrote an article in 1972 stating that after reading her programme during the interval of 'Gone With The Wind' at Drury Lane she spotted in the small print that the trainer of the wonderful horse was Miss Joan Rosaire. So it is not surprising that within a short time Irene was on her way to Billericay to interview Joan. On arrival there was banging going on in a shed, it was her father Ted 'a man who can do anything' says Joan. Ted then appeared with his wife, Zena who was once an aerial acrobat in the famous Rosaire Circus along with Joan who must be the warmest-hearted, rosiest, healthiest redhead imaginable.

Joan goes on to say: - 'I bought Charlie specially and trained him and sold him to Mr Fielding who produced the play. He was handed over on the opening night but I still retain authority over him and complete control and either my mother, Tracy or I go up every night for the performance. In fact, Harve Presnell, who plays Rhett Butler, stands there every night close to Charlie. Harve has been very good; he's a horseman himself and rodeo rider and he understand. I couldn't have been luckier and June Ritchie, Scarlett, has been wonderful too, because it's quite terrifying to sit up on that cart with all the commotion going on – and she isn't a horsewoman.'

Joan also explained to Irene that Charlie is a remarkable horse, with a marvellous temperament. 'Nothing shakes him although he has a mind of his own and can be very standoffish. I don't know what sort of life he led but he wouldn't eat sugar at first and wouldn't be patted but now he thinks he's rather good. He takes sugar and he likes Harve and June. He has his likes and dislikes among the cast – the actors and people who come up to talk to him each night and from being a poor old nag he's become terribly aristocratic. That's what I like, that an animal should develop its own character.'

Irene goes on to explain that the Rosaire estate rambles over acres studded with caravans used as bases by circus people from all over the world. There are enclosed paddocks and in one of them is star-performing Goldy, Joan's brilliant conquest and close companion, a Palomino eleven-year-old which listens and obeys in spite of a wild and wilful temperament, finding ways of expression not open to doubt. 'Goldy is incredible' says his mistress, 'a born professional.' Joan calls, Goldy comes and in a small training enclosure, he will be a rocking horse, will smile, whisper, pick up a towel and wipe Joan's face, cross his feet and leap to paw the air.

Goldy goes all over the country with Joan, he has a very beautiful understudy living in a separate paddock and will peep out to see Silver getting all the attention and will at once begin to show off.

They all have great fun at Willoughby Farm and you come away with one absolute certainty – the link between animal and trainer is without doubt a bond of love.

It is therefore not surprising that a report appeared in 'The World's Fair' December 1973 under the heading 'Pretty Girls' and this is what they had to say about our Joan: - 'Then of course horses, proud horses and more horses. Bred, fed, matched and plumed to perfection, tutored, trained and presented by the one and only Miss Joan Rosaire who has no equal in the circus world today and is my idea of the mistress of the horse.' (Reproduced by kind permission of the World's fair.)

Joan and Goldy were now in great demand. Engagements at home and abroad included sixteen weeks with Ken Dodd at the Royal Court Theatre, Liverpool in 1975. It started off as a ten week show but it went so well it was extended to sixteen weeks. The stables were about four miles away at Chilwell and nearby was the Vicarage car park where the horsebox was parked up.

Joan had been told that the owner of the Grand National Champion Red Rum had heard about her and this marvellous horse Goldy and wanted to come and see the show but there were no seats available. So she had a quiet word with Ken who immediately made available one of the private Box Seats.

Joan also remembers very clearly that both she and Tracy would ride onto the stage, Tracy on Johnny and Joan on Goldy (Silver). Both horses had Rawhide boots with rubber soles on so that they would not slip on the stage but on this occasion one of Goldy's boots came off. Joan stopped immediately, Tracy immediately knew what had happened, walked Johnny off, got off and gave the horse to a stage hand and promptly took one of his boots off, walked back on the stage bent down picked up Goldy's leg and placed the boot over its heel, luckily both horses had the same size boots.

Joan was quick to act and said 'here comes the maid' and then asked Goldy 'are you okay' who shook his head to say yes. What really amused Joan is that Tracy had not realised that on bending down to put the boot on her bottom was facing the audience. They are still not sure to this day whether the audience were aware that it was not part of the act. After the show Ken came up to them and thanked them for acting so fast. As they both said he was a gentleman and at Christmas time bought all the ladies perfume.

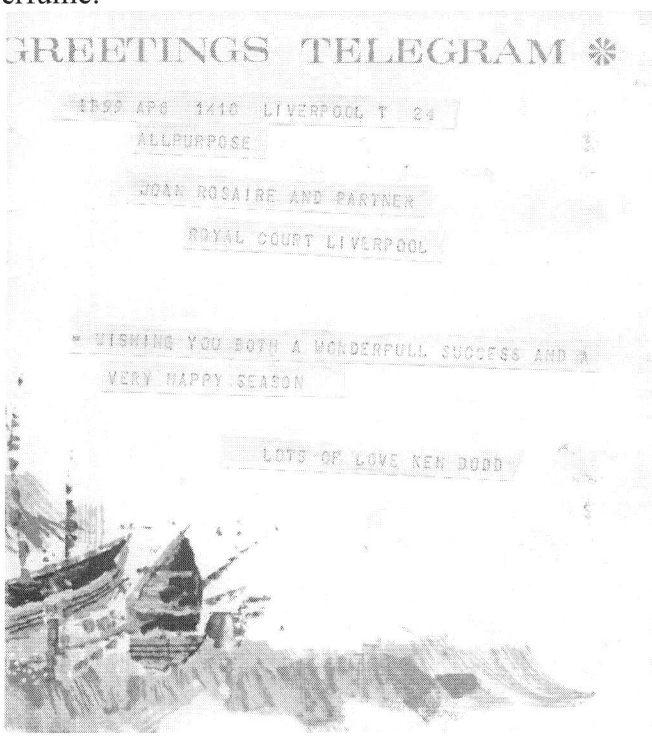
GREETINGS TELEGRAM

1899 AP8 1410 LIVERPOOL T 24
ALLPURPOSE

JOAN ROSAIRE AND PARTNER
ROYAL COURT LIVERPOOL

WISHING YOU BOTH A WONDERFULL SUCCESS AND A
VERY HAPPY SEASON

LOTS OF LOVE KEN DODD

Greetings Telegram from Ken Dodd

There were a few other embarrassing situations at other venues. There was the time that on one of her performances Joan wore a strapless toto made for her by her mother. Joan had not practised in it and as soon as Joan appeared on stage it slipped down. Joan though red in the face managed to correct her attire and continue with the show as if nothing had happened. No doubt the audience were quite amused.

Then there was the time she was wearing a white wig in the circus ring and Goldy pulled it off. Silver was also not short in getting up to mischief and on another occasion pulled her earring out and stood on her foot at the same time but one of the most amusing situations was when one of the Goldys ran across the ring and bit Joan – Joan's mike was on and the audience heard her shout out 'bugger off you bit me.' The question is did the audience realise it was not part of the act?

While at the shows, they would meet up with a number of friendly people who took them out for some lovely meals and were often allowed to their homes and have a bath instead of relying on the bucket of water back at the stables. So, though they really enjoyed the time they worked with Ken Dodd, they never got to bed until at least one in the morning after taking the horses back and settling them into riding stables at Chilwell. The problem was that Ken's show invariably overran and Joan, Tracy and the horses had to be in the finale. The laughter kept them going but with twice-nightly shows and having to be up at 6am there's no wonder they got exhausted and in the end they could not wait to get back to Billericay for a rest. Joan stayed in touch with Ken until he died.

Goldy appeared in a number of other shows with walk-on parts but in a Rolf Harris show Ken Dodd was sitting on Goldy and Rolf Harris was sitting on a chair close to the horse with the idea of painting Ken Dodd but the joke was that he was so close that he only painted his leg. The horse also appeared in the Generation Game with Bruce Forsyth and in Paul Daniel's magic show.

During this period, Joan's mother Zena was taken ill from which she never recovered. Joan had relied so much on the unfailing help and guidance of her mother and the loss was bitter indeed. It said much for Joan's courage and stamina that she was able to carry on so bravely and so successfully at this sad time in her life.

Although devoted to the circus arena and circus horses, Joan also had interests outside the circus and as we know had an early enthusiasm for show jumping which produced several successes including the North of England Championship for juvenile riders.

Poster

Tracy on Johnny

Goldy (Silver) and Joan performing in the Ken Dodd Show

She enjoyed running the riding school with her circus horses and had an abiding interest in dressage and 'Haute Ecole' in fact this led to the rare distinction of an offer of sponsorship to train in Vienna with one of the Spanish Riding School Oberberieter (chief rider) but the lure of the circus and an interest in training and presenting other types of animals proved too strong, so Joan stayed at home and continued to train and present all kinds of animal acts.

During this time, she acquired a good knowledge of equine ailments and occasionally wished she had been a vet. This enabled her to acquire a good knowledge of human disorders and this is what probably helped Joan get an assistant's job with a local doctor.

After the death of her mother Joan only occasionally accepted long seasonal engagements but preferred making short solo appearances in a variety of venues. This gave her the opportunity to spend more time at home with her father to whom she had always been devoted. Family ties have always been strong with the Rosaires. Joan idolized that most loveable of men, her grandfather, the Count Rosaire and always loved and admired her grandmother.

One such local event was on a brilliant, sunny but very chilly Sunday afternoon in the winter when she performed in front of a large crowd at an Essex riding centre event being organised by the Ragwood Riding Centre and South Essex Dressage from Benfleet. Joan opened her programme by explaining the origins and history of the circus in England. Then she demonstrated her skills by lungeing a three year old pony, belonging to the centre. The pony had never seen Joan before, let alone the other 100 or so people watching and had never been lunged. In a very short time, Joan and pony were friends and it was obediently trotting round on either rein and occasionally giving a little leap. (Lungeing is a technique for training horses, where a horse is asked to work at the end of a lunge line and respond to commands from a handler on the ground who holds the line – it is performed in a large circle with the horse travelling around the outside edge of a real or imaginary ring with the trainer in the middle.)

Silver and Joan at a local event, possibly a carnival

Joan then brought in one of her own horses and demonstrated her training methods. Then came Goldy who counted, agreed and disagreed with Joan empahatically nodding and shaking his head and pirouetted and finally showing their versatility they performed Dressage to Music.

She also remembers performing in Laindon in a field opposite the Laindon Shopping Centre, this was probably the field behind the Laindon Hotel that over the years had held various fetes and would have been the field that Billy Foyle's horse 'King' had performed his football skills in. Joan's act did not only include Goldy (Silver) but also her German Shepherd cross-breeds whose routines were sitting on a table, running in and out of Joan's legs as she walked, jumping through hoops and skip jumping over ropes etc.

As the 1970s rolled on the circuses began to change, circus animals were not wanted so often although Joan was still in demand for one off or short term performances. Tracy was beginning to think beyond the circus world. Though she loved horses she was very interested in heavy haulage Lorries, so she decided in her spare time to take HGV class one artic driving lessons. This she did through 'Benders' of Laindon and finally passed her test at her third attempt.

Joan training the dogs at the farm.

Then in 1979 at the age of 23 and after spending fifteen amazing years with Joan and the horses, Tracy decided with heavy heart that it was time to move on to pastures new. So, she went back home to spend more time with her parents and make new friends including boyfriends. It goes without saying that she obtained a lorry driving job with National Carriers at Kings Cross, London. Joan as you can imagine like Gaye and others before was terribly upset but fully understood her reasons for wanting to move on. There were a few years before they were in touch again but like Gaye they now speak fairly regularly, reminiscing about the good old days.

At the end of the 1970 season cousin David Rosaire (Hawkes) who had just finished a season at the Tower Circus, Blackpool contacted Joan and asked her if she would train some dogs to ride a pony in an act he had planned but did not have time. Joan was more than happy to help out. 'We had two big poodles ideal for making riding dogs and they seemed to enjoy it but the act would work better if there were three, one each on a pedestal and one on the pony. Training was going reasonably well, when David remembered that he had a cross-breed called "Pepay" that he had taught to ride and I could use him. Although I did practice with him he did not seem very keen.

Joan with the Dog Act

Well the opening night came and the dogs worked reasonably well, the riding part was a huge success. In fact my new horse was great, so I was feeling pretty good. David telephoned later to see how things went, I explained that all went well. He said, why not use Pepay occasionally. Reluctantly I agreed and at the next performance I used him and he performed better than I had hoped for but whilst taking our call, Pepay jumped onto the nearest knee that just happened to be a gentleman in a very smart navy-blue suit, leaving him smothered in lovely long hair. I immediately retrieved him, apologising profusely. Thankfully the gentleman was a good sport and took it in good spirit. I vowed to lynch David the next time I encountered him. Needless to say by the time I did meet him all was forgiven, though not forgotten.'

There was another occasion when Joan was performing with Chippy at Quilters School, Billericay. On the four corners of the field were P.A. speakers. Joan was in the middle of the field with Chippy, the act was going pretty well but then all of a sudden Chippy jumped off a pedestal and started to run over to one of the P.A. speakers, with Joan shouting 'where are you going'. Chippy had heard her voice come out of the speaker and it was off. Joan followed with 'Oi' 'come back here.' Chippy eventually responded and returned; the audience did not realise it was not part of the act.

Another of Joan's close circus friends is Tom Roberts who was part of the famous Roberts Brothers Circus. He first met Joan in the late 1970s at Belle Vue Manchester when he was working with elephants and horses. He got to know Joan very well and eventually asked her if she would show him how to train horses. Joan was normally reluctant to show others her secret as she put it - as far as Joan was concern her act was a secret. Tom however was different and she did take him under her wing and show him a few tricks. In Manchester at the time was Norman Barratt a close friend of Joan's. After a day's work whether it was a circus day or working around the circus looking after the animals Joan would have the pair around to her caravan/horsebox in the evening and cook them an evening meal.

At the time the Robert Brothers had a least twenty horses in addition to other animals and if Joan was not appearing for them they used to hire the horses out to other venues and Joan would often present them.

Later on, when Tom had passed his driving test, he bought himself a little mini and on one occasion Tom loaned the keys to Joan so she could go into the nearby town. Unfortunately, she backed it into a post she had not seen. She was obviously very apologetic when returning the car. Tom took it away, got it repaired and immediately gave Joan the keys. Tom is still in constant touch with Joan and normally refers to her as the oldest Rosaire alive.

In 1980 Joan met Julie Stott through a mutual friend's BBQ in Billericay. As Julie was working, she initially only went to the farm at weekends to help out but in 1991 partly because of her love of animals she started working there full time. So, in addition to mucking out around the farm she helped out at the various shows.

One Gala in particular Julie remembers was at Kings Lynn. On the way the lorry broke down at Luton. The lorry had to be completely emptied and Joan had to bleed the brakes. When they got close to the venue, they had to do it all over again and they only just managed to get to the venue on time. That was not the end of their troubles because when they got there, they found the area in at least 6 inches of water. The scouts who were there to control the car parks etc found their sleeping bags floating in their tents. They managed to find a small area that was not so wet to set up an arena with ropes but they could not get the speakers to work. Joan had to shout. Finally, every time Goldy (Sunny) walked around the area he would 'buzz' a small lad, who found it very funny. In fact, considering the situation the audience, Joan and Julie enjoyed the afternoon. Carl, Julie's husband became her accountant.

In June 1981 Joan performed for the League of Friends in a one day show in aid of the Royal Liverpool Children's Hospital at Myrtle Street. The profits of the show were for life-supporting medical equipment.

Joan's beloved father Ted Bunning died on the 25 November 1985 and the following is Joan's obituary of him that appeared in the March 1986 King Pole magazine: -

'My father was born on 6 August 1904 at Walsoken Manor, Walsoken, Norfolk. He was the proprietor of a garage and coachbuilders' business when he met the Rosaires. He subsequently sold the business and joined the circus, married my mother Zena in the Isle of Man and I am the only offspring (can you wonder?)! Dad maintained and built all the equipment for Count Rosaire until he retired and then Dad with brother-in-law's Dennis and Ivor continued with Circus Rosaire until both Ivor and Dennis left, leaving my father to run the show alone until 1956 when, for financial reasons, Dad decided to retire from circus life and settle down on our premises in Billericay. He resumed his coach building business until retired. He built my horseboxes, four of them and I believed he pioneered the 'Lived-in' horsebox that many of the showjumpers of today travel with. He also designed and built props, notably Gina's moon and rocket, Fossett's elephant tubs, lion cages, etc, too many to mention and living wagons for Jim and Sally Clubb, John Roberts and many travellers (fairgrounds) as well as my cousins Leonie Owles and Roy Shufflebottom. He was greatly liked and respected by the local farming fraternity, who brought their combined harvesters and the like to be mended. He always found time to help anyone who needed it, never talked about himself and was a very quiet and unassuming man but with a wickedly dry sense of humour!! He always gave me the greatest help and encouragement. He did appear briefly in the ring in the early days but preferred the management side of the circus. He was very good at handling all animals but was seldom credited for doing so. He always looked after my animals for me in my absences. He

is buried with my mother in the family plot at Brentwood. Thank you for remembering him, he was a truly remarkable man.'

In 1986 a local journalist visited Joan and was taken in by the amazing bond between her three magnificent Goldys, with their dun-coloured coats with pale silk-yellow manes and tails glowing in the sunlight and Joan as usual was not backward in showing them off.

Ted Bunning with Goldy (Silver)

Joan unlocks their stalls with her explaining that they need to be good locks as anything else they find easy to undo. She leads Silver out first into the lungeing arena, he curls his neck round hers, gives her a long-toothed grin, asking for an advance payment in the form of mints and then proving how laid back he is by nonchalantly crossing his legs. Duke follows, snorting with joy to unlock the gate to the lungeing arena with his nose. He briefly turns himself into a Polo pony with a crunch and gulp of mint and sets off on a Spanish walk with the proud leg lift from the shoulder rather than the knee. Out the corner of your eye you see Joan's own shoulder move. It's no more than a twitch, but it is one of the signals that is instantly obeyed. The tiniest of Joan's rocking movements triggers Duke's pirouettes, then like a firecracker he leaps into the air with delight.

Newcomer Trampas doesn't get his chance to show his genius, as Joan says, 'He is the cleverest horse you've ever seen but he is also a bit of a juvenile delinquent.'

Trampas being nosey at front gate - 1978

It was at Belle Vue, Manchester that Trampas made his first ring appearance, Norman Barrett came into the ring on Johnny to introduce Joan and Trampas. Unfortunately, other performers decided to get a better view of Joan's performance with her new Goldy and climbed on the wooden roof over the entrance, a spot where they could get a good view without the audience seeing them. Instead of walking quietly across the wooden roof they made a lot of tapping noise. This immediately disturbed Trampas and he promptly dumped Joan on the floor but being the professional she was, she immediately got back on the horse and went on with the routine as if nothing had happened. Trampus never did it again.

While the horses were taking centre stage 'Sain' a half Alsatian Joan had acquired, weaved tail wagging around the horses as she sang 'How Much is That Doggy in the Window.'

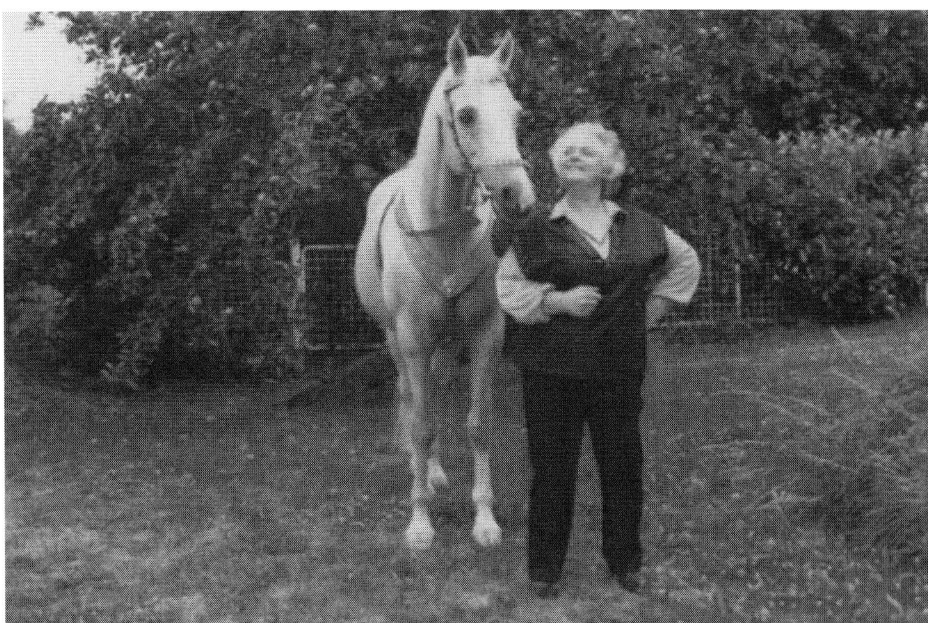

Trampas and Joan in her back garden.

Trampas Good Boy

Trampas waiting for his titbit

Trampas giving Joan a kiss

As you would have gathered there have been many highlights in Joan's career but none more than when she appeared to perform with Goldy at the Royal Variety Performance, London Palladium on 21st November 1988 in front of Queen Elizabeth, The Queen Mother and Princess Margaret. The overall show was hosted by Ronnie Corbett and Bruce Forsyth with guest appearances from Cliff Richard, Bob Monkhouse, Kylie Minogue and many others but it was the closing performance that was unusual, ending as it did with a spectacular circus finale hosted by Paul Daniels which included Joan performing with Goldy, with confetti and sparkling gold dust raining down on the stalls and balloons cascading from the roof. As one commentator remarked, '*scenes like this are commonplace on political rallies in the USA but it was the first time that the audience at a Royal Variety Performance had seen anything quite like it.'*

Joan on occasions would loan her horses out - one such occasion in August 1992 was when she lent Goldy out to Rose English though Joan as usual would be in the wings keeping an eye on the proceedings. Rose wrote, directed and performed her own work. She also performed along with other co-performers such as musicians, dancers, circus performers and horses. On this occasion she appeared at London's Queen Elizabeth Hall and in the second half of her act she presented her horse 'Mathematics' (alias Goldy). Joan although in the wings appeared at the final curtain call and as various news reports stated deserved to take a large share of the credit. Other venues included Sadler's Wells and Theatre Royal, Brighton.

As already mentioned, Joan appeared on TV several times, there was one particular occasion during the early 1990s where she appeared with Goldy in an episode of 'Natural History Museum.' They were discussing animal behaviour. On the show was a Ron Austin who believed his horse was capable of independent abstract thought. He was getting his horse to count by lifting or tapping his foot by following written instructions on a card leaving everybody to believe that the horse on its own was capable of carrying out the instruction. They had not accounted for Joan being there who noticed that Ron was inadvertently raising his eyebrows when showing the horse, the card with numbers on it.

So, they did the experiment again but this time the horse had blinkers on so he could not see the individual's face and as Joan expected the horse did not respond. Joan then performed a routine with Goldy where the making of several slight movements such as a twitch of her shoulder were Goldy's cue to perform. The professor's eyebrow movement was his horse's cue. Joan also explained that horses do however, understand a few words such as yes and no and would nod their heads accordingly.

S

Horse tapping out the number

In November 1993 Joan agreed to put on a 'Rosaire Road Show' at the Equestrian Centre in Dry Street Langdon Hills, Essex only a few miles from her Billericay home, the centre has since moved to a new site at Barleyland Farm just a few miles away. Joan agreed to do the event on the understanding that she received half the takings, an arrangement she often agreed too.

The following is a report by Nick Leggett in King Pole Magazine, March 1994: -

'Twas the coldest night of the year – Joan had invited me to see "The Rosaire Road Show" which was being held at the Longwood Equestrian Centre at 8.00 p.m. "Come to my little bash" I had been told. As I drove there feeling like the proverbial brass monkey, I had visions this indeed might be a "little bash", the weather had been very unkind but to my surprise the supporters had turned up, in fact so many the car park was full and the queue went right around the centre.

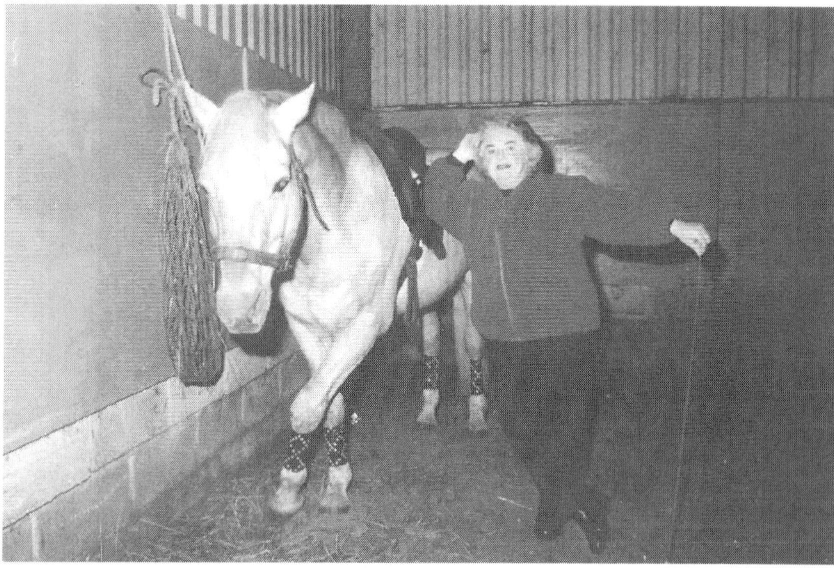

Joan and Goldy at Longwood waiting to perform

Joan's cousin Leonie was on the door doing a great job of getting the public in out of the cold. Hot food and drinks were on hand to warm the patrons. Seating was at a premium, people "perched" wherever possible until, in true circus style, bales of straw were requisitioned as extra seating. The outstanding response to the show is surely a tribute to a wonderful lady and horsewoman.

The Programme was as follows: -

Introduction. Brief intro about Joan, Circus Rosaire, showing TV commercials etc. A welcome with good favourable comments about circus animals and training. Assisting Joan was the "horse parlour maid," Julie Stott who was making a video for an education pack.

Initial training of the liberty horse. Training a three, rising four-year-old show pony deliberately unseen by Joan in order to prove what could be achieved in a very short space of time. Working the long lunge, changing direction, the call, kneeling. Further training. This time with a show pony only seen six or seven times. This training featured direction, call, kneeling, pirouettes, pedestal, Spanish walk etc.

Canine capriole everyone's favourite, the dogs, rollover, skipping, begging, pedestal work, counting and singing and dogs being just dogs much to the amusement of the crowd, especially the children.

Musical ride by "La Fiesta de Las Romeras". A very good colourful ride with great Spanish costumes featuring mounted quadrilles, carousel, serpentine, etc., all to a very high standard performed by Sharon Hamlin and friends (the ride was conceived by Joan using Sharon's show ponies).

Intermission – more warm coffee.

Haute Ecole, High school – Joan, unable to ride due to back and leg problems, Sharon Hamlin had been press-ganged and thrown in at the deep end. This was Joan's normal Haute Ecole act as seen on many circuses in the past, but always worth seeing again.

Goldy. What can one say apart from should it read "Goldy presents Joan". This act demonstrated the great bond between animals and handler – an act superb. This was a fitting climax to the show. Any Questions. Many were forthcoming even if it was getting late which only proves the interest this workshop had engendered. Photo call with press and birthday children.

Unfortunately, I was unable to see Joan at the end but listening to the comments as I left of horse owners and public alike this "little bash" was a huge success.'

Joan was not only called upon to give performances but often asked to give talks to various groups such as the Women's

Institute. In March 1998 David Davis who was President of the Circus Friends Association invited Joan to give a talk on her life and that of Goldy at their AGM in Sheffield. Unfortunately, David discovered later it was not recorded.

In 1996 Nell Gifford made several visits to see Joan to pick up a few tricks in training horses. Joan was happy to do this but as she says 'I never showed anybody Goldy's act.' Nell must have been happy with the advice Joan gave as she says Joan is a lovely woman. At the time Nell had been working in several circuses in particular acting as ring-mistress for Santus Circus in France.

Nell obviously had signs of owning her own circus and soon after she met her future husband 'Toti' they put on their first show in 1999. So, by 2000 the Gifford's Circus was up and running. It is based on the 1930s theme, so it is one of the few circuses in Britain that still perform with domestic animals, horses, dogs and birds. There are about thirty circuses in Britain but only a couple perform with domestic animals.

Joan had given up trick riding many moons ago because of the pain caused by injuries to her knees, exasperated following a riding incident with Frank Paulo where Joan was thrown off and her leg landed underneath her and went crack. She could not get up and was carried to the caravan. Zena gave her compresses of vinegar and salt and sent her back into the ring with Goldy who soon became aware of her plight - in fact instead of pushing Joan out of the ring he walked beside her. As you would expect from such an accident it was her cartilages that had been damaged but it was not until the late 1990s that her knees really started to play up and eventually in 1998, she went under the knife and had a knee joint replacement. This resulted in her giving up horse riding but she was still able to work her horses from the floor, though her performing days were reduced. In 1999 she suddenly received a call from cousin David in Florida and all he said was 'I need you'. Joan flew out not knowing what he wanted her to do. When show time came, Joan still did not know what she was to do until David met her with a big baboon who immediately got hold of Joan's trousers. David said 'just sit there quietly for a moment'. The baboon jumped up and put his arms around her neck. David's reponse 'She likes you'. 'Now will you take it up to the coach that is in the ring'. The coach was full of dogs waiting to be pulled by a great spotted dane and all he was waiting for was his rider. So Joan did exactly as she was told, walked in with the baboon who promptly got on the coach and took hold of the reins. An experience Joan has never forgotten.

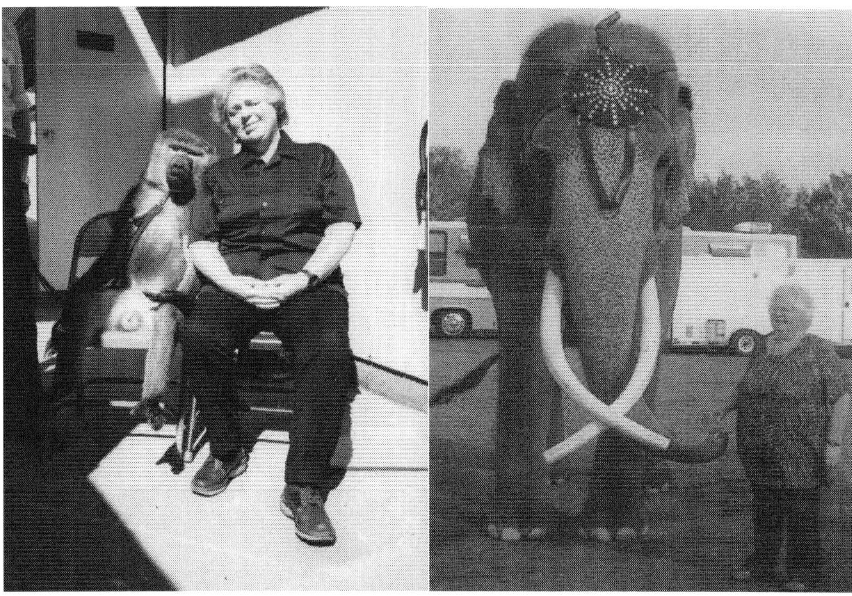

Joan looks quite happy with the baboon but it was one of her most scary moments though she looks more worried with the elephant.

Joan's horses as you would expect would need shoeing every now and again and this was down to Vic Welch the local Dunton blacksmith. He would visit the farm in his van carrying a portable anvil and fire to carry out the job. If he was unable to,

Joan would walk at least three horses at a time to the blacksmiths shop to have them shoed (3 miles away).

The following are a few more memories from local people who remember the circus and Joan with affection:

Jack Bartlett - Local Billericay postman remembers the roar of animals as he came past the farm. 'I came face to face with a friendly bear one morning when delivering,' he recalled. The bear had somehow unchained himself and seemed to be smiling at Jack who was more than scared of those grinning teeth.

Trevor Baylis - Sylvia Kent in an article back in 2014 reported on an interview she had with Trevor when he told her of wanting to join Circus Rosaire.

He said: 'I arrived in Billericay as a youngster keen on joining that particular circus. I was then a stuntman and underwater performer. When I arrived in Billericay to audition, I remember viewing the cages for the menagerie where a collection of animals were housed for the winter.

Here I remember meeting the beautiful Joan Rosaire and immediately fell in love with her and have included her in my autobiography, along with my wonderful memories of the town of Billericay. I often wonder how things would have turned out if I had gone on to become a circus performer.'

It would have been sometime in the early 1950s when Trevor Baylis arrived at Billericay with his friend Johnny Pugh and his father who was known as Digger. Digger was an Australian circus entrepreneur who sorted out lavish circus promotions. He had come to audition an act he wanted for the Sunderland Empire variety bill. It was an Ali Baba routine in which a girl writhed with a snake while dancing to languorous music. Digger liked what he saw and offered forty pounds for the week as long as the snake did not misbehave as they had just redecorated the dressing rooms.

Trevor as you would have gathered did not follow a career in the circus but later in life became an inventor, his main invention being the 'wind up radio'. He was awarded the OBE in 1997 and the CBE in 2014.

Joan as you can imagine met literally hundreds of people, Trevor being one of them but it is Johnny Pugh she remembers more clearly with affection as he performed with the Rosaire Circus at Bridlington on the trampoline.

Anita Mills - Billericay Community Archive (24 June 2013) – 'Wonderful memories from Willoughby Farm Riding School seeing all the animals from the circus who came for the winter and watching the performers practising on the trapeze. I think I was lucky to have been a part of it and will always remember Joan Rosaire she was my hero!'

Daren Keen - Billericay Community Archive (2 September 2013) – 'My grandfather (Bill Hutchins) owned the nursery next to the winter quarters in Coxs Farm Road. I remember Joan well and used to cut her front grass as a boy to earn extra pocket money. My family were also connected to the winter quarters as my Father's (Clive Kean) side were circus people who used to stay there. My parents met this way.'

Rick Colebrook - Billericay Community Archive (15 July 2015) – 'I worked with Joan at the American Adventure in 1989 in Silver City and it was a great pleasure to be part of her show and I remember Goldy as well, my stage name was J.D. McQuade.'

Colin Humphrey - Laindon Community Archive - (8 May 2018) – 'I can't be sure of the exact year but it would have been sometime in the early 1970s. I was working as field service engineer for a company called Vision Hire, I was based in Billericay and covered an area between Ingatestone, Stock, Wickford and the Bursteads. On one occasion I received a call to attend to a faulty television in a large caravan parked up in a farmyard off Cox's Farm Road. In the yard there were a number of caravans and large Lorries. I can recall that once I had entered the caravan my attention was drawn to a large open topped cardboard box and something inside the box was moving about quite vigorously. I initially thought that it probably contained puppies, the lady who lived in the caravan could see that I was curious so she bade me to have a look, to my amazement inside the box there were two beautiful lion cubs. I was allowed to stroke them before getting on with the task that took me there in the first place.'

Bert French – Remembers Joan with affection following her visit to Watch House Farm in Wash Road to collect hay and straw for the animals. Joan also remembers him as a real gentleman and the fact that his father George often went in the Dukes Head, Billericay and had the odd pint with the Count. George was on the Billericay District Council and was one of the main instigators of the Government accepting the need for Basildon to have a new town built within its boundaries to overcome its massive infrastructure problems in addition to helping those bombed out in London.

You would have gathered by now that Joan did not only perform and train horses but was also licenced to train and perform with lions, elephants, llamas, bulls, zebras, camels, pigs, dogs, monkeys, geese etc not forgetting that she performed in her early career on the trapeze and trampoline. A circus person through and through.

If by any chance Joan found herself with very little to do which was not often, she would indulge in another of her hidden talents – drawing!

Memories of one day tenting – drawing by Joan.

Joan's Clowns

Another piece of Joan's Handiwork

Finally, the World's Fair magazine reported that the circus fans of the world have said that Joan's act with Goldy is the only one of its kind performed by a woman since the seventeen hundreds.

Promotional Die-Cast Models

Chapter 6 - Final Curtain Call

As you would expect I visited Joan on many, many occasions slowly picking away at her memories. There was also a cup of tea and biscuits or cakes waiting for me. We would sit and chat and if I was lucky, I would come away with a little more information to add to the book. We would sit in her narrow caravan-shape kitchen. The seats we would sit on were bus seats though upholstered and the table was from a local store, all obtained by her father. We would then occasionally venture into her front room and other rooms in the bungalow to see the array of horse and circus books and photos situated on top of her furniture or adorning the walls, highlighting a testimony to her nomadic origins.

The kitchen then broadens into a conservatory which was not out of bounds to her horses. Beyond you can still see the small buildings and workshops used for storing big top equipment during the winter season. You can also see the stables and circular lungeing arena where the uncanny links between Joan and her Goldy's were forged. Beyond there is eight acres of land which is now rented out.

After the death of Joan's father in 1985 she stayed on in the bungalow and though she had a number of suitors she never married saying: - 'It's probably true what they say about horsewomen - that we're domineering, I wouldn't have wished myself on any man form that reason.'

The farm on the death of Joan's father was transferred to Carlos and Joan and they sold it at about the time Joan gave up performing. It is now a small industrial site.

'I travelled alone, with only my horses as company. Horses were my life and there were times I would go mad if I didn't have them to chat to…like when I was touring North Africa. There was just me and my horses for miles between towns. My Goldy horses were my family, I lived for them and they live for me.'

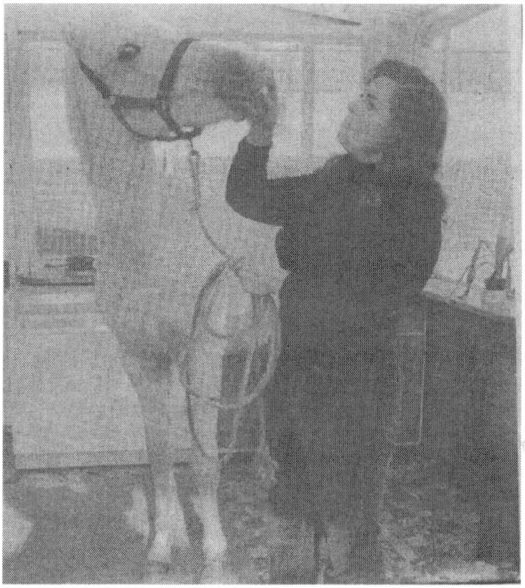

Goldy (Trampus) in the conservatory.

Silver demonstrating his Esther Ranzen impersonation

When Joan talked, her animals listened and usually acted. If she told her pet dog to close the door behind her off he would trot and do so. If she asked Goldy to mark four and do an Esther Rantzen impersonation, the lips would curl back and the teeth come jutting out. There was no threat in her voice, no 'big stick attitude. Just a polite request. Joan's talent for teaching animals to perform tricks was truly remarkable.

Joan in an unusual attire, no wonder she had many suitors.

The King Pole magazine edition September 2000 reports on Joan and Goldy's farewell public performance on Sunday 16 July at the Steam Rally and Country Fair in the grounds of St Edmund's College, between Ware and Puckeridge, Hertfordshire. 'Joan was assisted by Julie Scott and her husband Carl. Joan told the audience that both she and her Goldys were now retiring. Needless to say, they gave a sparkling performance, which was entertaining for the general public and they gave a magical indication of affinity between two friends, one human and the other equine.

Trampas, Duke and Sunny will continue to live with Joan at her Billericay farm. Sunny as you would have gathered was the last of the Goldys. He was not as bright as the others in fact he often got nervous in front of the public. The first time he actually went in front of the public he messed but when Joan asked him to apologise to the nice people who had come to see him, this he did by nodding his head.'

One of Joan's last performances at St Edmund's College with Silver.

However, Joan believes her last performance was a few months later at another Gala performance in a field somewhere off the A1. 'There was a very large crowd who had come to watch me, I thanked them all for coming to witness my last public performance and as I looked around many were crying and as you would expect I also had a tear in my eye.'

Many entertainers do not know when to retire and often have many last performances. Joan was no different but as she was approaching 70 felt it was time to hang up her saddle. I wonder how her horses felt.

Then in February 2001 approximately a year after Joan hung up her riding boots the World's Fair Newspaper held its third annual circus awards. Jeremy Beadle hosted the presentation and Paul Daniels and his wife Debbie Mcgee were guests of honour at the Reunion.

Bobby Roberts was presented with the Humanitarian Award 2000 by Paul Daniels. Malcolm Clay received the Circus Showman 2000 award on behalf of Martin Lacey Jnr. Laci Endresz was presented with the Professional Presentation of a Circus 2000 by Paul Daniels. Don Stacy received the World's Fair Service Award from Paul Daniels and Michael Mellor. The Animal Husbandry in Circus Award went to Joan's lifetime friend Tommy Roberts and Paul Daniels received a surprise presentation from Michael Mellor for Dedication in Support of the Circus.

The final and most prestigious award of the evening being the Lifetime Achievement Award went to none other than our Joan. Don Stacy had this to say about her: -

'The recipient this year I had described in World's Fair earlier this year as one of the kindest, most charming and most loved British artistes and concluded that "she is one of a kind" and most definitely 'One of Our Kind of People'. Soon after publication of that tribute, she was to retire after a lifetime in the circus world and a lifetime devoted to her precious animals. There is no more a staunch supporter of Circus and of circuses than Joan Rosaire and she made a happy choice for our Lifetime

Achievement Award this year and we were especially thrilled that, despite recent ill health, she was able to accept the award herself from Paul Daniels.'

This followed a two-page article on Joan's life by Don Stacy in the May 2000 World's Fair Newspaper.

Joan being presented with her Lifetime Achievement award by Paul Daniels.
Joan later gave the award to her cousin David in America.

In the years that followed Joan was asked along to many functions to give talks on her life in the circus and in 2007 she was asked to judge the 9th Circus World Championships. We are now in 2019 and wherever Joan goes, in the circus world she is enthusiastically welcomed and made a real fuss off.

It's time for Joan to have the last word: -

'I haven't got a qualification to my name but I knew my animals. I liked to call myself an animal teacher, not trainer because I took their natural tendencies and taught them how to adapt. Animal rights campaigners believe animals shouldn't be taught to perform tricks, they claim it is demeaning and unnatural. I am all for legislation which protects animals from abuse – but nobody loves animals more than me but you have to remember and respect their way of thinking and not give them your way of thinking.'

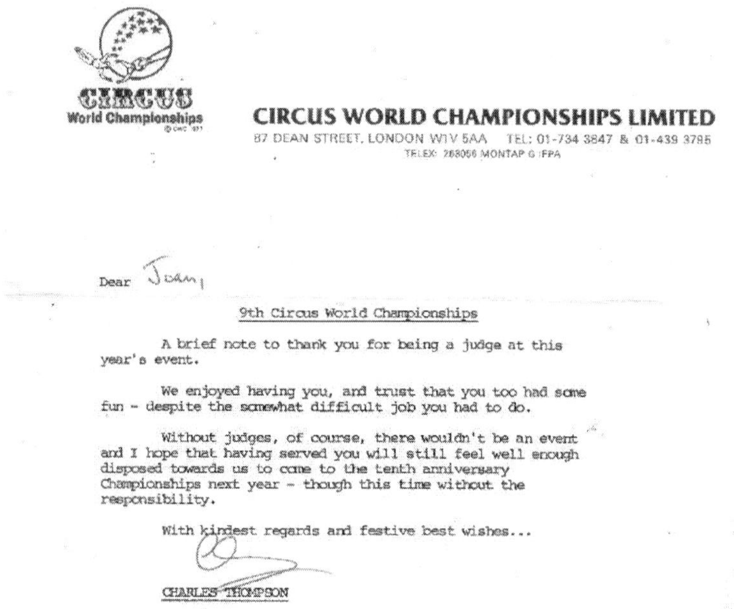

CIRCUS World Championships

CIRCUS WORLD CHAMPIONSHIPS LIMITED

87 DEAN STREET, LONDON W1V 5AA TEL: 01-734 3847 & 01-439 3785

TELEX: 268056 MONTAP G IFPA

Dear Joan,

9th Circus World Championships

A brief note to thank you for being a judge at this year's event.

We enjoyed having you, and trust that you too had some fun – despite the somewhat difficult job you had to do.

Without judges, of course, there wouldn't be an event and I hope that having served you will still feel well enough disposed towards us to come to the tenth anniversary Championships next year – though this time without the responsibility.

With kindest regards and festive best wishes...

CHARLES THOMPSON

'The way to teach animals is with reward and punishment (punishment was only the withholding of treats, until they carried out the task, then you rewarded them quickly) – the same as you teach humans. We are a high form of animal, that's all. You can't teach either animals or humans properly if you try to beat something into them, and you can't teach animals to like you.'

'My horses went everywhere with me, come rain or shine I looked after them, they were as important to me as humans, they were part of my family, I loved them and I think they loved me.'

Today with her horses gone she still does not feel lonely, next door is her cousin Susan and husband Ralph Bibby who keep a close eye on her. Alison a nearby neighbour and friend frequently calls and takes her out. She is also in constant contact with members of her family in America and there are a number of circus and other friends who ring and visit regularly.

'I admit that when I first retired, I bitterly regretted it but now I am happy with life. I still like to be associated with the circus world and after all these years I am extremely happy when I am recognised, it gives me much pleasure.

So, let me end with a comic ditty song, sung to me by Arthur Scott, which I feel sums me up. Arthur worked for a time with the circus.'

'I came here on purpose direct from the circus, to tell you the tale of my life.
I'm old and just a bit saucy and up to now nobody's wife,
I am queen and reign all alone, and the horse's backside is my throne it's a lonely old farrow I am trying to plough.
My friends are all pensioned or passed on by now,
And though I am nuts and a bit of a cow I am Joanie the circus queen.'

Chapter 7 - Circus Programmes and Posters.

A few more programmes and posters of some of the events where Joan and Goldy performed: -

JOAN ROSAIRE AND GOLDY

INDOOR OR OUTDOOR
CARNIVALS · CIRCUSES · RODEOS
CABARETS · THEATRES
HIGH SCHOOL DEMONSTRATIONS, ETC

Dear Friends,

We would like to offer you the opportunity to book Europe's leading Outdoor/Indoor Attraction.

Absolutely unique - a top animal act featuring the horse that can do just about everything - even talk! A decidedly different kind of act that will be enjoyed by the whole family.

We are sublimely confident that GOLDY THE WONDER HORSE will be a tremendous attraction at your function.

Also introducing SHARN, Joan's remarkable pet dog. Sharn has many attributes, she has mastered the complexities of arithmetic and is also a top class singer.

SOME OF THEIR APPEARANCES

BBC1 and 2
ITV Commercials
Ken Dodd Spectacular
Rolph Harris Show
Max Bygraves Singalong
Bruce Forsyth Generation Game
Numerous Childrens Shows
Paul Daniels Magic Show
Leading Caberts
Discovery of Animal Behaviour
Horse of the Year Show, Wembly
Royal International Horse Show, Olympia
Demonstrations at Leading Riding and Training Establishments

Circuses
Blackpool Tower
Billy Smarts
Chipperfields
Belle View, Manchester
Kelvin Hall, Glasgow
Cirque de Hiver, Paris
Cirque Medrano, Paris
Cirkus Knie, Switzerland
Circo Americano, Spain

REQUIREMENTS

A suitable fenced arena approximately 40 foot in diameter, with a microphone reaching all parts of the arena, (preferably a radio microphone), a cassette deck. We have our own tapes.

Parking for a large horsebox.

Terms:

MELBOURNE, COXES FARM ROAD, BILLERICAY, ESSEX CM11 2UB ☎ BILLERICAY 0277 624972

Rosaire Programme – late 1940s – Is this our Joan?

Another programme from the 1940s Bilston -
with Jim Parson as ringmaster

Bouglione Programme – Joan opens the programme in the first half by presenting a Cavalry display and then reappears in the final act of the second half before the final parade to perform with Goldy -

Coronation Programme – Bridlington 1953

Billy Russell's Circus at the Great Yarmouth Hippodrome - 1966

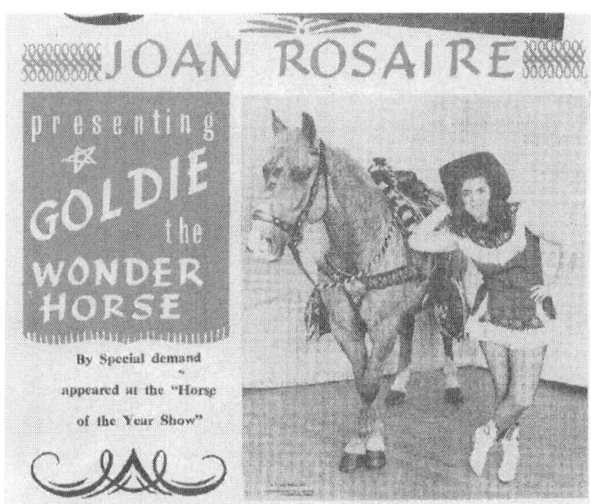

Inside page – Yarmouth 1966

Programme reads 'Goldy the Wonder Horse' with his partner Joan Rosaire. – Have you ever seen an educated horse? If not here is your chance, for Goldy is a horse in a million. Assisted by his charming partner Joan Rosaire. Goldy shows you how intelligent he is, much to everyone's delight.

Joan as usual appearing with Goldy with Tracy assisting – 1977

Inside Caption – A decidedly different animal act featuring the horse that can do just about everything – even talk! But you'll have to see the show to discover just how….

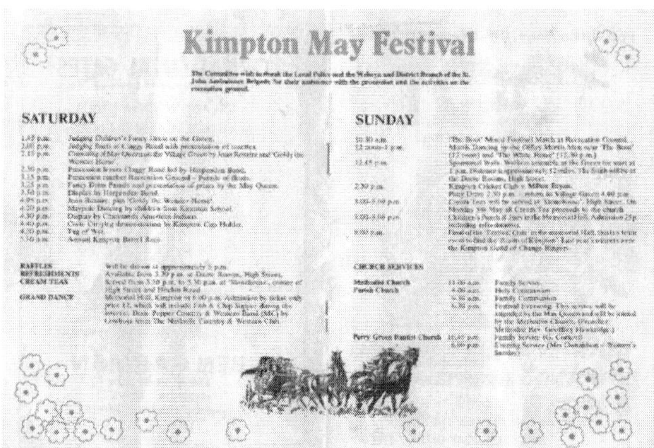

Inside message – Welcome to Kimpton on this our 16th celebration of the May Festival. – This year the committee accepted the suggestion that the theme should be the 'American Wild West' and we are pleased that Joan Rosaire with 'Goldy the Wonder Horse' will be crowning our May Queen - 1980

Belle Vue Circus included acts from all over the World – Sweden, France, Germany, USA, Italy, Taiwan and of course our Joan and Goldy from Great Britain- 1981

Joan and Goldy just seemed to appear everywhere and on this occasion they had two slots.

Inside Caption: - Joan Rosaire reckons Goldy can do just about anything…even talk. This nine year old Palomino has appeared all over Britain with Joan and was invited to a recent Horse of the Year show.

Gerry Cottle's Circus presented by Jeremy Beadle – surprisingly the second half we see that Jeremy Beadle was being presented by Goldy the Wonder Horse and Joan – 1992/3

Joan's own poster

Joan this time with Tracy

JOAN ROSAIRE
AND
GOLDY
THE WONDER HORSE

B.B.C T.V. — I.T.V.
★
HORSE OF THE YEAR SHOW — WEMBLEY
★
BILLY SMARTS CIRCUS
★
BLACKPOOL TOWER CIRCUS
★
CIRQUE DE HIVER — PARIS
★
CIRQUE MEDRANO — PARIS
★
CIRKUS KNIE — SWITZERLAND
★
CIRCO AMERICANO — SPAIN
★
LEADING CABARETS

A top animal act featuring the horse that can do just about everything but talk. A decidedly different kind of act that will be enjoyed by the whole family. If you want novelty you are going to get your chance when you see the amazing Joan Rosaire and Goldy.

SUITABLE FOR INDOOR OR OUTDOOR • CARNIVALS
CIRCUSES • RODEOS • CABARETS • THEATRES, Etc.

Joan Rosaire Phone: BILLERICAY 4972
WILLOUGHBY FARM · COXES FARM ROAD · BILLERICAY · ESSEX

Another one of Joan's leaflets advertising the various circuses etc. where she has performed

Chapter 8 - Photo Gallery

Joan on Firefly 1946 – first horse bought herself.

Joan at the farm

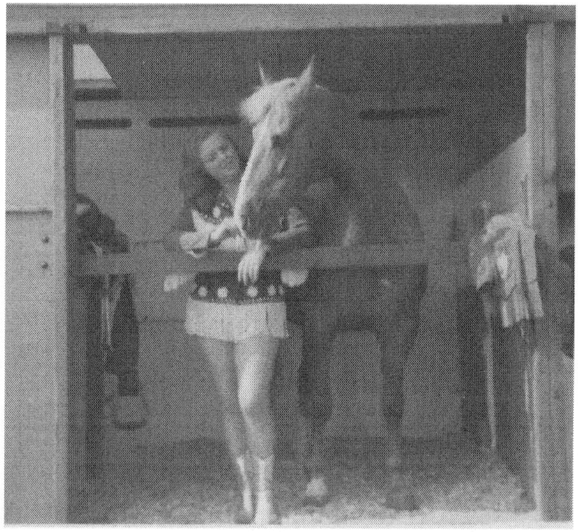

Joan and Goldy in the stables at the farm

Tishy Joan's first pony misbehaving

Goldy in practice at home catching the cloth from Joan

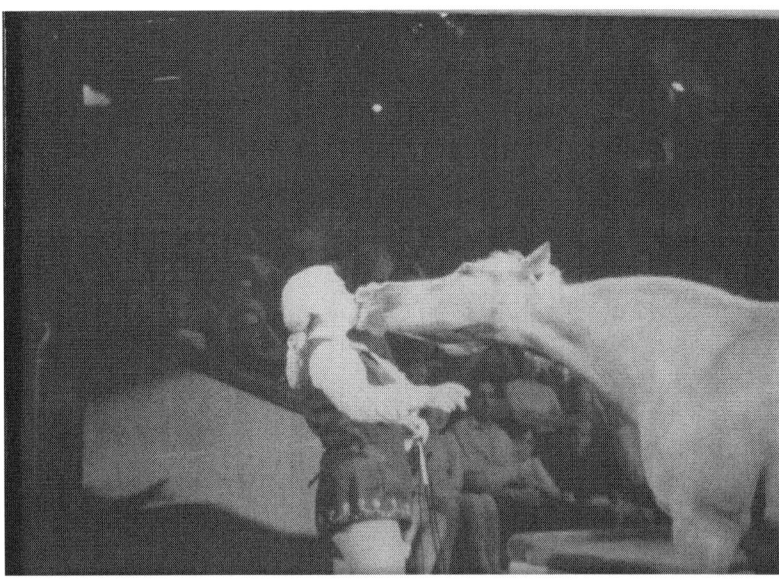

Kisses from Goldy

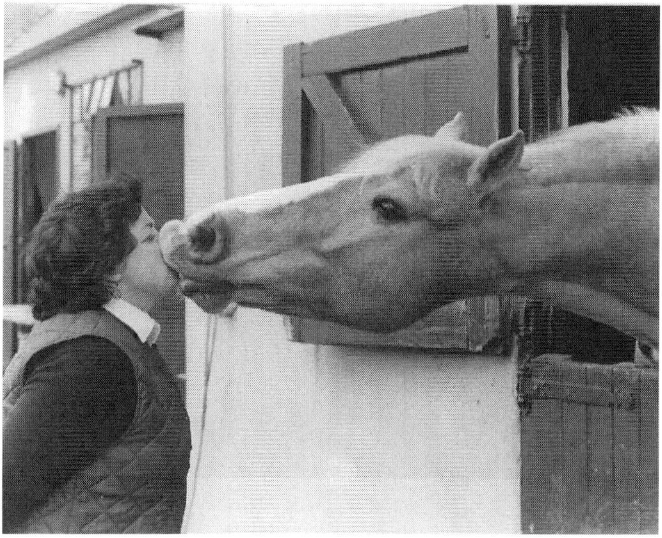

More kisses galore from Silver

Joan and Goldy

Joan in her cowboy outfit and a painting of her on Goldy

Joan performing with Luis and Klenn just two more of the many horses she worked with.

Luis on his own

Joan on Stage with Goldy

Joan and Goldy in the Channel Islands

Looks like Goldy is getting a telling off from Joan

Joan with 'John Wellington – Wells' (Johnny) –her arab stallion on which she did High School and also occasionally the Goldy Act

Silver taking Joan's coat off

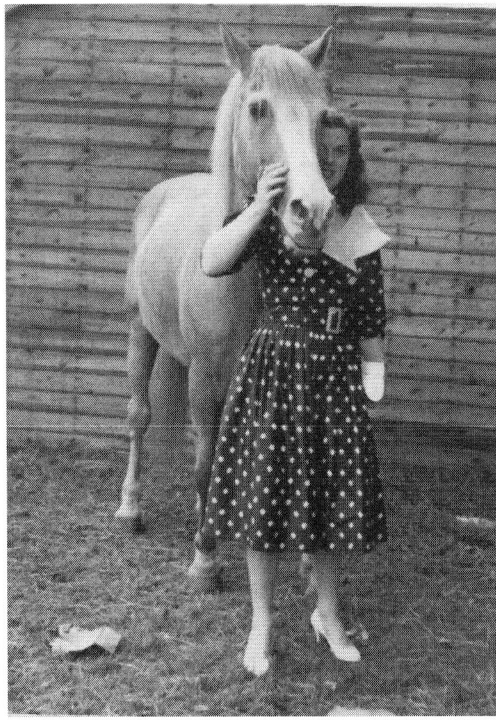

Joan and Tony (Derrick's Horse)

Joan and the llama

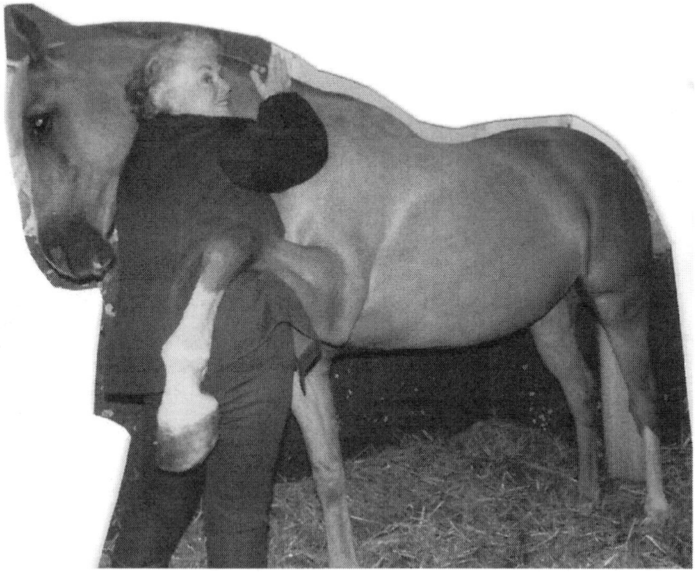

Silver - how about a cuddle?

Trampus, Silver and Duke with Joan on the farm

Joan with others on the beach at Blackpool – Whenever they were in Blackpool they exercised the horses on the beach and gave them a paddle.

Silver

This photo in colour was given to Joan Rosaire as a gift on 3rd August 2006 – by Tracy.

"To the greatest Horse Trainer of all time."

Photo taken in 1966 at a circus in France.

References

www.circuswonderland.com
The Happy Highways by Rupert Croft-Cooke
The Circus Has No Home by Rupert Croft-Cooke
Bowers Bugle
Burning Bright by Tracy Chevalier
Beneath the Big Top by Steve Ward
Chris Barltroop – www.centreforcircusculture.eu
Circus Tails by Joan Rosaire, Jack Niblett and Muriel Farnden
Daily Telegraph – The Third Book of Obituaries – Entertainers
Bandwagon (Newsletter) – August 1957
Billericay Community Archive
British Library – Oral History of the Circus – Joan Rosaire
British Newspapers archive
Circus – A World History by Rupert Croft-Cooke and Peter Cotes
David Davis – Vice President of Circus Friends Association
Financial Times
King Pole Magazine
Laindon and District Community Archive
Lucky Rider Magazine
www.Circopedia.org– Short History of the Circus.
www.wikipedia
Gazette
Essex Chronicle
Essex Newsman
The Stage (Weekly newspaper)
Trevor Baylis, autobiography – 'Clock This' – my life as an Inventor
Sylvia Kent – Blog – sylviakent.blogspot.com
World's Fair Magazine
Woman's Weekly – article by Irene Heath-1972